Charles Sangster

Hesperus

And Other Poems And Lyrics

Charles Sangster

Hesperus
And Other Poems And Lyrics

ISBN/EAN: 9783744704397

Printed in Europe, USA, Canada, Australia, Japan

Cover: Foto ©Thomas Meinert / pixelio.de

More available books at **www.hansebooks.com**

HESPERUS,

AND

Other Poems and Lyrics.

BY CHARLES SANGSTER,

AUTHOR OF "THE ST. LAWRENCE AND THE SAGUENAY, AND OTHER POEMS."

Montreal:
JOHN LOVELL, ST. NICHOLAS STREET.

Kingston:
JOHN CREIGHTON, KING STREET.
1860.

THESE

Poems and Lyrics

ARE

DEDICATED

TO

My Niece,

CARRIE MILLER,

OF

SANDWICH, C. W.

CONTENTS.

vi CONTENTS.

CONTENTS.

POEMS.

DEDICATORY POEM.

Dear Carrie, were we truly wise,
And could discern with finer eyes,
    And half-inspired sense,
    The ways of Providence :

Could we but know the hidden things
That brood beneath the Future's wings,
    Hermetically sealed,
    But soon to be revealed :

Would we, more blest than we are now,
In due submission learn to bow,—
    Receiving on our knees
    The Omnipotent decrees ?

That which is just, we have.   And we
Who lead this round of mystery,
    This dance of strange unrest,
    What are we at the best ?—

Unless we learn to mount and climb ;
Writing upon the page of time,
    In words of joy or pain,
    That we've not lived in vain.

We all are Ministers of Good;
And where our mission's understood,
How many hearts we must
Raise, trembling, from the dust.

Oh, strong young soul, and thinking brain!
Walk wisely through the fair domain
Where burn the sacred fires
Of Music's sweet desires!

Cherish thy Gift; and let it be
A Jacob's ladder unto thee,
Down which the Angels come,
To bring thee dreams of Home.

What were we if the pulse of Song
Had never beat, nor found a tongue
To make the Poet known
In lands beyond his own?

Take what is said for what is meant.
We sometimes touch the firmament
Of starry Thought—no more;
Beyond, we may not soar.

I speak not of myself, but stand
In silence till the Master Hand
Each fluttering thought sets free.
God holds the golden key.

KINGSTON, C. W., *May 1st*, 1860.

HESPERUS:

A LEGEND OF THE STARS.

———

PRELUDE.

The Stars are heaven's ministers;
    Right royally they teach
God's glory and omnipotence,
    In wondrous lowly speech.
All eloquent with music as
    The tremblings of a lyre,
To him that hath an ear to hear
    They speak in words of fire.

Not to learnèd sagas only
    Their whisperings come down;
The monarch is not glorified
    Because he wears a crown.
The humblest soldier in the camp
    Can win the smile of Mars,
And 'tis the lowliest spirits hold
    Communion with the stars.

Thoughts too refined for utterance,
    Ethereal as the air,
Crowd through the brain's dim labyrinths,
    And leave their impress there;

As far along the gleaming void
    Man's tender glances roll,
Wonder usurps the throne of speech,
    But vivifies the soul.

Oh, heaven-cradled mysteries,
    What sacred paths ye've trod—
Bright, jewelled scintillations from
    The chariot-wheels of God !
When in the spirit He rode forth,
    With vast creative aim,
These were His footprints left behind,
    To magnify His name !

———

We gazed on the Evening Star,
    Mary and I,
    As it shone
    On its throne
      Afar,
    In the blue sky;
Shone like a ransomed soul
In the depths of that quiet heaven;
    Like a pearly tear,
    Trembling with fear
On the pallid cheek of Even.

And I thought of the myriad souls
Gazing with human eyes
    On the light of that star,
    Shining afar,
In the quiet evening skies;

Some with winged hope,
　Clearing the cope
Of heaven as swift as light,
　Others, with souls
　Blind as the moles,
Sinking in rayless night.

Dreams such as dreamers dream
　　Flitted before our eyes ;
　　　Beautiful visions !—
　　　Angelo's, Titian's,
　　Had never more gorgeous dyes :
We soared with the angels
　　Through vistas of glory,
We heard the evangels
　　Relate the glad story
　　Of the beautiful star,
　　Shining afar
　　In the quiet evening skies.

And we gazed and dreamed,
Till our spirits seemed
　　Absorbed in the stellar world ;
Sorrow was swallowed up,
Drained was the bitter cup
Of earth to the very lees ;
And we sailed over seas
　　Of white vapour that whirled
　　Through the skies afar,
Angels our charioteers,
Threading the endless spheres,

And to the chorus of angels
Rehearsed the evangels
The Birth of the Evening Star.

———

I.

Far back in the infant ages,
Before the eras stamped their autographs
Upon the stony records of the earth;
Before the burning incense of the sun
Rolled up the interlucent space,
Brightening the blank abyss;
Ere the Recording Angel's tears
Were shed for man's transgressions:
A Seraph, with a face of light,
And hair like heaven's golden atmosphere,
Blue eyes serene in their beatitude,
Godlike in their tranquillity,
Features as perfect as God's dearest work,
And stature worthy of her race,
Lived high exalted in the sacred sphere
That floated in a sea of harmony
Translucent as pure crystal, or the light
That flowed, unceasing, from this higher world
Unto the spheres beneath it.   Far below
The extremest regions underneath the Earth
The first spheres rose, of vari-coloured light,
In calm rotation through aërial deep,
Like seas of jasper, blue, and coralline,
Crystal and violet; layers of worlds—
The robes of ages that had passed away,

Left as memorials of their sojournings.
For nothing passes wholly. All is changed.
The Years but slumber in their sepulchres,
And speak prophetic meanings in their sleep.

FIRST ANGEL.

Oh, how our souls are gladdened,
When we think of that brave old age,
When God's light came down
From heaven, to crown
Each act of the virgin page !

Oh, how our souls are saddened,
At the deeds which were done since then,
By the angel race
In the holy place,
And on earth by the sons of men !

Lo, as the years are fleeting,
With their burden of toil and pain,
We know that the page
Of that primal age
Will be opened up once again.

II.

Progressing still, the bright-faced Seraph rose
From Goodness to Perfection, till she stood
The fairest and the best of all that waked
The tuneful echoes of that lofty world,
Where Lucifer, then the stateliest of the throng
Of Angels, walked majestical, arrayed

In robes of brightness worthy of his place.
And all the intermediate spheres were homes
        Of the existences
        Of spiritual life.
Love, the divine arcanum, was the bond
That linked them to each other—heart to heart,
And angel world to world, and soul to soul.
        Thus the first ages passed,
        Cycles of perfect bliss,
God the acknowledged sovereign of all.
Sphere spake with sphere, and love conversed with love,
From the far centre to sublimest height,
And down the deep, unfathomable space,
To the remotest homes of angel-life,
A viewless chain of being circling all,
And linking every spirit to its God.

ANGEL CHORUS.

        Spirits that never falter,
        Before God's altar
Rehearse their pæans of unceasing praise;
        Their theme the boundless love
        By which God rules above,
        Mysteriously engrafted
        On grace divine, and wafted
Into every soul of man that disobeys.

        Not till the wondrous being
        Of the All-Seeing
Is manifested to finite man,
        Can ye understand the love

By which God rules above,
Evermore extending,
In circles never-ending,
To every atom in the universal plan.

SECOND ANGEL.

Oh, the love beyond computing
　Of the high and holy place!
　The unseen bond
　Circling beyond
The limits of time and space.

Through earth and her world of beauty
The heavenly links extend,
　Man feels its presence,
　Imbibes its essence,
But cannot yet comprehend.

THIRD ANGEL.

But the days are fast approaching,
　When the Father of Love will send
　His interpreter
　From the highest sphere,
That man fully may comprehend.

III.

Oh, truest Love, because the truest life!
Oh, blest existence, to exist with Love!
Oh, Love, without which all things else must die
The death that knows no waking unto life!
Oh, Jealousy that saps the heart of Love,

And robs it of its tenderness divine;
And Pride, that tramples with its iron hoof
Upon the flower of love, whose fragrant soul
Exhales itself in sweetness as it dies!
A lofty spirit surfeited with Bliss!
A Prince of Angels cancelling all love,
All due allegiance to his rightful Lord;
Doing dishonour to his high estate;
Turning the truth and wisdom which were his
For ages of supreme felicity,
To thirst for power, and hatred of his God,
Who raised him to such vast preëminence!

SECOND ANGEL CHORUS.

Woe, woe to the ransomed spirit,
　　Once freed from the stain of sin,
　　　　Whose pride increases
　　　　Till all love ceases
　　To nourish it from within!
Its doom is the darkened regions
Where the rebel angel legions
Live their long night of sorrow;
Where no expectant morrow,
　　No mercy-tempered ray
　　From the altar of to-day,
Comes down through the gloom to borrow
One drop from their cup of sorrow,
　　Or lighten their cheerless way.

FIRST ANGEL.

But blest be the gentle spirit
    Whose love is ever increased
        From its own pure soul,
        The illumined goal
    Where Love holds perpetual feast!

IV.

       Ingrate Angel, he,
To purchase Hell, and at so vast a price!
'Tis the old story of celestial strife—
Rebellion in the palace-halls of God—
False angels joining the insurgent ranks,
Who suffered dire defeats, and fell at last
From bliss supreme to darkness and despair.
But they, the faithful dwellers in the spheres,
Who kept their souls inviolate, to whom
Heaven's love and truth were truly great rewards:
For these the stars were sown throughout all space,
As fit memorials of their faithfulness.
The wretched lost were banished to the depths
Beneath the lowest spheres.   Earth barred the space
Between them and the Faithful.   Then the hills
Rose bald and rugged o'er the wild abyss;
The waters found their places; and the sun,
The bright-haired warder of the golden morn,
Parting the curtains of reposing night,
Rung his first challenge to the dismal shades,
That shrunk back, awed, into Cimmerean gloom;
And the young moon glode through the startled void
With quiet beauty and majestic mien.

SECOND ANGEL.

Slowly rose the dædal Earth,
    Through the purple-hued abysm
    Glowing like a gorgeous prism,
Heaven exulting o'er its birth.

Still the mighty wonder came,
    Through the jasper-coloured sphere,
    Ether-winged, and crystal-clear,
Trembling to the loud acclaim.

In a haze of golden rain,
    Up the heavens rolled the sun,
    Danae-like the earth was won,
Else his love and light were vain.

So the heart and soul of man
    Own the light and love of heaven;
    Nothing yet in vain was given,
Nature's is a perfect plan.

V.

The glowing Seraph with the brow of light
Was first among the Faithful. When the war
Between heaven's rival armies fiercely waged,
She bore the Will Divine from rank to rank,
The chosen courier of Deity.
Her presence cheered the combatants for Truth,
And Victory stood up where'er she moved.
And now, in gleaming robe of woven pearl,
Emblazoned with devices of the stars,
And legends of their glory yet to come,

The type of Beauty Intellectual,
The representative of Love and Truth,
She moves first in the innumerable throng
Of angels congregating to behold
The crowning wonder of creative power.

THIRD ANGEL CHORUS.

Oh, joy, that no mortal can fathom,
To rejoice in the smile of God!
To be first in the light
Of His Holy sight,
And freed from His chastening rod.
Faithful, indeed, that soul, to be
The messenger of Deity!

FIRST ANGEL.

This, this is the chosen spirit,
Whose love is ever increased
From its own pure soul,
The illumined goal
Where Love holds perpetual feast.

VI.

With noiseless speed the angel charioteers
In dazzling splendour all triumphant rode;
Through seas of ether painfully serene,
That flashed a golden, phosphorescent spray,
As luminous as the sun's intensest beams,
Athwart the wide, interminable space.
Legion on legion of the sons of God;
Vast phalanxes of graceful cherubim;

Innumerable multitudes and ranks
Of all the hosts and hierarchs of heaven,
Moved by one universal impulse, urged
Their steeds of swiftness up the arch of light,
From sphere to sphere increasing as they came,
Till world on world was emptied of its race.
Upward, with unimaginable speed,
The myriads, congregating zenith-ward,
Reached the far confines of the utmost sphere,
The home of Truth, the dwelling-place of Love,
Striking celestial symphonies divine
From the resounding sea of melody,
That heaved in swells of soft, mellifluous sound,
To the blest crowds at whose triumphal tread
Its soul of sweetness waked in thrills sublime.
The sun stood poised upon the western verge;
The moon paused, waiting for the march of earth,
That stayed to watch the advent of the stars;
And ocean hushed its very deepest deeps
    In grateful expectation.

SECOND ANGEL.

Still through the viewless regions
    Of the habitable air,
        Through the ether ocean,
        In unceasing motion,
Pass the multitudinous legions
    Of angels everywhere.

Bearing each new-born spirit
    Through the interlucent void

To its starry dwelling,
Angel anthems telling
Every earthly deed of merit
To each flashing asteroid.

THIRD ANGEL.

Through the realms sidereal,
Clothed with the immaterial,
Far as the fields elysian
In starry bloom extend,
The stretch of angel vision
Can see and comprehend.

VII.

Innumerable as the ocean sands
The angel concourse in due order stood,
In meek anticipation waiting for
The new-created orbs,
Still hidden in the deep
And unseen laboratory, where
Not even angel eyes could penetrate :
A star for each of that angelic host,
Memorials of their faithfulness and love.
The Evening Star, God's bright eternal gift
To the pure Seraph with the brow of light,
And named for her, mild Hesperus,
Came twinkling down the unencumbered blue,
On viewless wings of sweet melodious sound,
Beauty and grace presiding at its birth.
Celestial plaudits sweeping through the skies
Waked resonant pæans, till the concave thrilled

Through its illimitable bounds.
With a sudden burst
Of light, that lit the universal space
As with a flame of crystal,
Rousing the Soul of Joy
That slumbered in the patient sea,
From every point of heaven the hurrying cars
Conveyed the constellations to their thrones—
The throbbing planets, and the burning suns,
Erratic comets, and the various grades
And magnitudes of palpitating stars.
From the far arctic and antarctic zones,
Through all the vast, surrounding infinite,
A wilderness of intermingling orbs,
The gleaming wonders, pulsing earthward, came;
Each to its destined place,
Each in itself a world,
With all its coming myriad life,
Drawing us nearer the Omnipotent,
With hearts of wonder, and with souls of praise:
Astrea, Pallas, strange Aldebaran,
The Pleiads, Arcturus, the ruddy Mars,
Pale Saturn, Ceres and Orion—
All as they circle still
Through the enraptured void.
For each young angel born to us from earth,
A new-made star is launched among its peers.

FULL ANGEL CHORUS.

Dreamer in the realms aërial,
Searcher for the true and good,

Hoper for the high, ethereal
Limit of Beatitude,
Lift thy heart to heaven, for there
Is embalmed thy spirit prayer :
Not in words is shrined thy prayer,
But thy Thought awaits thee there.
God loves the silent worshipper.
The grandest hymn
That nature chants—the litany
Of the rejoicing stars—is silent praise.
Their nightly anthems stir
The souls of lofty seraphim
In the remotest heaven.   The melody
Descends in throbbings of celestial light
Into the heart of man, whose upward gaze,
And meditative aspect, tell
Of the heart's incense passing up the night.
Above the crystalline height
The theme of thoughtful praise ascends.
Not from the wildest swell
Of the vexed ocean soars the fullest psalm ;
But in the evening calm,
And in the solemn midnight, silence blends
With silence, and to the ear
Attuned to harmony divine
Begets a strain
Whose trance-like stillness wakes delicious pain.
The silent tear
Holds keener anguish in its orb of brine,
Deeper and truer grief
Than the loud wail that brings relief,

As thunder clears the atmosphere.
But the deep, tearless Sorrow,—how profound !
Unspoken to the ear
Of sense, 'tis yet as eloquent a sound
As that which wakes the lyre
Of the rejoicing Day, when
Morn on the mountains lights his urn of fire.
The flowers of the glen
Rejoice in silence ; huge pines stand apart
Upon the lofty hills, and sigh
Their woes to every breeze that passeth by ;
The willow tells its mournful tale
So tenderly, that e'en the passing gale
Bears not a murmur on its wings
Of what the spirit sings
That breathes its trembling thoughts through all the
        drooping strings.
He loves God most who worships most
In the obedient heart.
The thunder's noisome boast,
What is it to the violet lightning thought ?
So with the burning passion of the stars—
Creation's diamond sands,
Strewn along the pearly strands,
And far-extending corridors
Of heaven's blooming shores ;
No scintil of their jewelled flame
But wafts the exquisite essence
Of prayer to the Eternal Presence,
Of praise to the Eternal Name.
The silent prayer unbars

The gates of Paradise, while the too-intimate,
Self-righteous' boast, strikes rudely at the gate
Of heaven, unknowing why it does not open to
Their summons, as they see pale Silence passing
    through.

VIII.

In grateful admiration, till the Dawn
Withdrew the gleaming curtains of the night,
We watched the whirling systems, until each
Could recognize their own peculiar star;
       When, with the swift celerity
       Of Fancy-footed Thought,
The light-caparisoned, aërial steeds,
       Shod with rare fleetness,
Revisited the farthest of the spheres
Ere the earth's sun had kissed the mountain tops,
Or shook the sea-pearls from his locks of gold.

————

      Still on the Evening Star
      Gazed we with steadfast eyes,
         As it shone
         On its throne
           Afar,
      In the blue skies.
      No longer the charioteers
      Dashed through the gleaming spheres;
      No more the evangels
        Rehearsed the glad story;
      But, in passing, the angels
        Left footprints of glory:

For up the starry void
Bright-flashing asteroid,
Pale moon and starry choir,
Aided by Fancy's fire,
Rung from the glittering lyre
Changes of song and hymn,
Worthy of Seraphim.
Night's shepherdess sat, queenlike, on her throne,
Watching her starry flocks from zone to zone,
While we, like mortals turned to breathing stone,
Intently pondered on the Known Unknown.

CROWNED.

Her thoughts are sweet glimpses of heaven,
  Her life is that heaven brought down;
Oh, never to mortal was given
  So rare and bejewelled a crown!
I'll wear it as saints wear the glory
  That radiantly clasps them above—
    Oh, dower most fair!
    Oh, diadem rare!
  Bright crown of her maidenly love.

My heart is a fane of devotion,
  My feelings are converts at prayer,
And every thrill of emotion
  Makes dearer the crown I would wear.
My soul in its fulness of rapture
  Begins its millennial reign,
    Life glows like a sun,
    Love's zenith is won,
  And Joy is sole monarch again.

My noonday of life is as morning,
  God's light streams approvingly down;
Uncovered, I wait her adorning,
  She comes with the beautiful crown!
I'll wear it as saints wear the glory
  That radiantly clasps them above—
    Oh, dower most fair!
    Oh, diadem rare!
  Bright crown of her maidenly love.

MARILINE.

I.

At the wheel plied Mariline,
Beauteous and self-serene,
Never dreaming of that mien
Fit for lady or for queen.

Never sang she, but her words,
Music-laden, swept the chords

Of the heart, that eagerly
Stored the subtle melody,
Like the honey in the bee ;
Never spake, but showed that she

Held the golden master-key
That unlocked all sympathy

Pent in souls where Feeling glows,
Like the perfume in the rose,
Like her own innate repose,
Like the whiteness in the snows.

Richly thoughted Mariline !
Nature's heiress !—nature's queen !

II.

By her side, with liberal look,
Paused a student o'er a book,
Wielder of a shepherd's crook,
Reveller by grove and brook :

Hunter-up of musty tomes,
Worshipper of deathless poems :

Lover of the true and good,
Hater of sin's evil brood,
Votary of solitude,
Man, of mind-like amplitude.

With exalted eye serene
Gazed he on fair Mariline.

Swifter whirled the busy wheel,
Piled the thread upon the reel—   .
Saw she not his spirit kneel,
Praying for her after-weal?

Like the wife of Collatine,
Busily spun Mariline.

III.

Hour by hour, and day by day,
Sang the maid her roundelay ;
Hour by hour, and day by day;
Spun her threads of white and gray.

While the shepherd-student held
Commune with the great of eld :

Pondered on their wondrous words,
While he watched his scattered herds,
While he stemmed the surging fords.
And he knew the lore of birds,

Learned the secrets of the rills,
Conversed with the answering hills.

Like her threads of white and gray,
Passed their mingled lives away,
One unceasing roundelay—
Winter came, it still was May!

IV.

When the spring smiled, opening up
Pink-lipped flower and acorn cup;

When the summer waked the rose
In the scented briar boughs;
When the earth, with painless throes,
Bore her golden autumn rows—

Field on field of grain, that pressed,
Childlike, to her fruitful breast—

When hale winter wrapped his form
In the mantle of the storm,
Tamed the bird, and chilled the worm,
Stopped the pulse that thrilled the germ;

As the seasons went and came,
One in heart, and hope, and aim,

Cheered they each the other on,
Where was labor to be done,
At day-break or set of sun,
Like two thoughts that merge in one.

Dignified, and soul-serene,
Busily spun Mariline.

V.

Brightly broke the summer morn,
Like a lark from out the corn,—
Broke like joy just newly born
From the depths of woe forlorn,—

Broke with grateful songs of birds,
Lowings of well-pastured herds;

Hailed by childhood's happy looks,
Cheered by anthems of the brooks—
Chants beyond the lore of books—
Cawing crows, instead of rooks.

Glowed the heavens—rose the sun,
Mariline was up, for one.

VI.

Like a chatterer tongue-tied,
Lo, the wheel is placed aside!—
Not from indolence or pride—
Mariline must be a Bride!

Fairest maid of maids terrene!
Bride of Brides, dear Mariline!

VII.

Up the meditative air
Passed the smoke-wreaths, white and fair,
Like the spirit of the prayer
Mariline now offered there:

Passed behind the cottage eaves,
Curling through the maple leaves :

Through the pines and old elm trees,
Relics of past centuries,
Hardy oaks, that never breeze
Humbled to their gnarly knees :

Forest lords, beneath whose sheen
Flowers bloomed for Mariline.

Round the cottage, fresh and green,
Climbed the vine, the scarlet bean,
Morning-glories peeped between,
Looking out for Mariline.

Odours never felt before
Tranced the locust at the door,

Vieing with the mignonette
Round the garden parapet,
Whose rare fragrances were met
By rich perfumes, rarer yet,

Stealing from the garden walks,
Sentineled with hollyhocks.

VIII.

What a heaven the cottage seemed !
Love's own temple, where Faith dreamed
Of the coming years that beamed
On them, as pale stars have gleamed

Through unnavigated seas,
To which the prophetic breeze

Whispered of a future day,
When swift fleets would urge their way,
Through the waters cold and gray,
Like the dolphins at their play.

There the future Bride, and he,
Prince of love's knight-errantry,

Whose good shepherd arms must hold
This pet yeanling of the fold,
Gift of God so long foretold,
Gift beyond the price of gold.

There the parents, aged and hale,
Passing down life's autumn vale,

With a joy as rare and true
As their daughter's eye of blue,
With such hopes as reach up to
Heaven's gate, when, passing through,

Peris, bound for higher skies,
Win the Celestial Paradise.

IX.

Thoughtfully stood Mariline,
Whitely veiled, and soul-serene;
Love's fair world for her demesne,
Never looked she more a queen—

With her maidens by her side,
Smiling on the coming bride.

Her pet lamb, with comic mirth,
Licked her hand and scampered forth;
The fine sheep-dog, on the hearth,
Kindly eyed her for her worth.

X.

Up the air, across the moor,
As they left the cottage door,

Chimed the merry village-bells,
Music-wrapt the neighbouring fells,
Stirred the heart's awakened cells,
Like fine strains from fairy dells.

Past the orchard, down the lane,
By fresh wavy fields of grain,

By the brook, that told its love
To the pasture, glen, and grove—
Sacred haunts, that well could prove
Vows enregistered above.

By the restless mill, where stood,
Bowing in his amplest mood,

The old miller, hat in hand,
Rich in goodness, rich in land,
On whose features, grave and bland,
Glowed a blessing for the band.

Through the village, where, behind
Many a half-uplifted blind,

Eyes, that might have lit the skies
Of Mahomet's Paradise,
Flashed behind the curtains' dyes,
With a cheerful, half-surprise.

Through the village, underneath,
Many a blooming flower-wreath,

Garlanding the arches green
Reared in honour of the queen
Of this day of days serene,
Day of days to Mariline.

To the church, whose cheering bells
Told the tale in music-swells—

Told it to the country wide,
With an earnest kind of pride—
Something not to be denied—
" Mariline must be a Bride !"

XI.

Up the aisle with solemn pace,
Meeting God there, face to face.

Never Bride more chaste or fair
Stood before His altar there,
Her ripe heart aflame with prayer,
Blessing Him for all His care :

Every earthly promise given,
Registered with joy in heaven.

From the galleries looked down,
Village belle and country clown,
Men with honest labour brown,
Far removed from mart or town :

Smiling with a zealous pride
On the shepherd and his bride—

Playmates of their early days;
For their walks in wisdom's ways,
Ever crowned with honoured bays
Of esteem and ardent praise.

XII.

Well done, servant of the Lord !
Grave expounder of His Word,

Who in distant Galilee
Graced the marriage feast, that He,
With all due solemnity,
Might commission such as thee

To do likewise, and unite
Souls like these in marriage plight.

With what manly, gentle pride,
The glad Shepherd clasps his Bride!
Love like theirs, so true and tried,
Ever true love must abide !

XIII.

Ye whose souls are strong and firm,
In whom love's electric germ

Has been fanned into a flame
At the mention of a name;
Ye whose souls are still the same
As when first the Victor came,

Stinging every nerve to life,
In the beatific strife,

Till the man's divinest part
Ruled triumphant in the heart,
And, with shrinking, sudden start,
The bleak old world stood apart,

Periling the wild Ideal
By the presence of the Real:

Ye, and ye alone, can know
How these twain souls burn and glow,
Can interpret every throe
Of the full heart's overflow,

That imparts that light serene
To the brow of Mariline.

THE HAPPY HARVESTERS.

A CANTATA.

I.

Autumn, like an old poet in a haze
Of golden visions, dreams away his days,
So Hafiz-like that one may almost hear
The singer's thoughts imbue the atmosphere;
Sweet as the dreamings of the nightingales
Ere yet their songs have waked the eastern vales,
Or stirred the airy echoes of the wood
That haunt the forest's social solitude.
His thoughts are pastorals; his days are rife
With the calm wisdom of that inner life
That makes the poet heir to worlds unknown,
All space his empire, and the sun his throne.
As the bee stores the sweetness of the flowers,
So into autumn's variegated hours
Is hived the Hybla richness of the year;
Choice souls imbibing the ambrosial cheer,
As autumn, seated on the highest hills,
Gleans honied secrets from the passing rills;
While from below, the harvest canzonas
Link vale to mountain with a chain of praise.
Foremost among the honoured sons of toil
Are they who overcome the stubborn soil;
Brave Cincinnatus in his country home
Was even greater than when lord of Rome.
Down sinks the sun behind the lofty pines
That skirt the mountain, like the straggling lines

Of Ceres' army looking from the height
On the dim lowlands deepening into night;
Soft-featured twilight, peering through the maze,
Sees the first starbeam pierce the purple haze;
Through all the vales the vespers of the birds
Cheer the young shepherds homeward with their
And the stout axles of the heavy wain   [herds;
Creak 'neath the fulness of the ripened grain,
As the swarth builders of the precious load,
Returning homewards, sing their Autumn Ode.

AUTUMN ODE.

God of the Harvest! Thou, whose sun
 Has ripened all the golden grain,
We bless Thee for Thy bounteous store,
The cup of Plenty running o'er,
 The sunshine and the rain.

The year laughs out for very joy,
 Its silver treble echoing
Like a sweet anthem through the woods,
Till mellowed by the solitudes
 It folds its glossy wing.

But our united voices blend
 From day to day unweariedly;
Sure as the sun rolls up the morn,
Or twilight from the eve is born,
 Our song ascends to Thee.

Where'er the various-tinted woods,
    In all their autumn splendour dressed,
Impart their gold and purple dyes
To distant hills and farthest skies
    Along the crimson west:

Across the smooth, extended plain,
    By rushing stream and broad lagoon,
On shady height and sunny dale,
Wherever scuds the balmy gale,
    Or gleams the autumn moon:

From inland seas of yellow grain,
    Where cheerful Labour, heaven-blest,
With willing hands and keen-edged scythe,
And accents musically blythe,
    Reveals its lordly crest:

From clover-fields and meadows wide,
    Where moves the richly-laden wain
To barns well-stored with new-made hay,
Or where the flail at early day
    Rolls out the ripened grain:

From meads and pastures on the hills,
    And in the mountain valleys deep,
Alive with beeves and sweet-breathed kine
Of famous Ayr or Devon's line,
    And shepherd-guarded sheep:

The spirits of the golden year,
From crystal caves and grottoes dim,
From forest depths and mossy sward,
Myriad-tongued, with one accord
Peal forth their harvest hymn.

II.

Their daily labour in the happy fields
A two-fold crop of grain and pleasure yields,
While round their hearths, before their evening fires,
Where comfort reigns, whence weariness retires,
The level tracts, denuded of their grain,
In calm dispute are bravely shorn again,
Till some rough reaper, on a tide of song,
Like a bold pirate, captivates the throng:

A SONG FOR THE FLAIL.

A song, a song for the good old Flail,
And the brawny arms that wield it,
Hearty and hale, in our yeoman mail,
Like intrepid knights we'll shield it.
We are old nature's peers,
Right royal cavaliers!
Knights of the Plough! for no Golden Fleece we sail,
We're Princes in our own right—our sceptre is the Flail.

A song, a song for the golden grain,
As it wooes the flail's embraces,
In wavy sheaves like a golden main,
With its bright spray in our faces.

Mirth hastens at our call,
Jovial hearts have we all!
Knights of the Plough! for no Golden Fleece we sail,
We're Princes in our own right—our sceptre is the Flail.

A song, a song for the good old Flail,
    That our fathers used before us;
A song for the Flail, and the faces hale
    Of the queenly dames that bore us!
        We are old nature's peers,
        Right royal cavaliers!
Knights of the Plough! for no Golden Fleece we sail,
We're Princes in our own right—our sceptre is the Flail.

III.

Fair was the maid, and lovely as the morn
From starry Night and rosy Twilight born,
Within whose mind a rivulet of song
Rehearsed the strains that from her lips ere long
Welled free and sparkling, as the vocal woods
Repeat the day-spring's sweetest interludes.
Her gentle eyes' serenest depths of blue
Shrined love and truth, and all their retinue;
The health and beauty of her youthful face
Made it the Harem of each maiden grace;
And such perfection blended with her air,
She seemed some stately Goddess moving there:
Beholding her, you thought she might have been
The long-lost, flower-loving Proserpine:

AN AUTUMN CHANGE.

" Oh, dreamy autumn days!
I seek your faded ways,
As one who calmly strays
  Through visions of the past ;
I walk the golden hours, .
And where I gathered flowers
The stricken leaves in showers
  Are hurled upon the blast."

Thus mused the lonely maid,
As through the autumn glade,
With pensive heart, she strayed,
  Regretting Love's delay ;
In vain the traitor flies!
To pleading lips and eyes,
Sweet looks, and tender sighs,
  He falls an easy prey.

" Oh, dreamy autumn days!
I tread your bridal ways,
As one who homeward strays,
  Through realms divinely fair ;
I walk Love's radiant hours,
Fragrant with passion flowers,
And blessings fall like dowers
  Down the elysian air."

Thus mused the maiden now,
With sunny heart and brow,
For Love had turned his prow

Towards the Golden Isles,
Where from Piercan springs
The soul of Music sings
Its sweet imaginings,
    Through all the Land of Smiles.

IV.

Up the wide chimney rolls the social fire,
Warming the hearts of matron, youth, and sire;
Painting such grotesque shadows on the wall,
The stripling looms a giant stout and tall,
While they whose statures reach the common height
Seem spectres mocking the hilarious night.
From hand to hand the ripened fruit went round,
And rural sports a pleased acceptance found;
The youthful fiddler on his three-legged stool,
Fancied himself at least an Ole Bull;
Some easy bumpkin, seated on the floor,
Hunted the slipper till his ribs were sore;
Some chose the graceful waltz or lively reel,
While deeper heads the chess battalions wheel,
Till some old veteran, compelled to yield,
More brave than skilful, vanquished, quits the field.
As a flushed harper, when the doubtful fight
Favors the prowess of some stately knight,
In stirring numbers of triumphal song
Upholds the spirits of the victor throng,
A sturdy ploughboy, wedded to the soil,
Thus sung the praises of the partner of his toil:

THE SOLDIERS OF THE PLOUGH.

No maiden dream, nor fancy theme,
   Brown Labour's muse would sing;
Her stately mien and russet sheen
   Demand a stronger wing.
Long ages since, the sage, the prince,
   The man of lordly brow,
All honour gave that army brave,
   The Soldiers of the Plough.
       Kind heaven speed the Plough!
       And bless the hands that guide it;
         God gives the seed—
         The bread we need,
       Man's labour must provide it.

In every land, the toiling hand
   Is blest as it deserves ;
Not so the race who, in disgrace,
   From honest labour swerves.
From fairest bowers bring rarest flowers,
   To deck the swarthy brow
Of those whose toil improves the soil,
   The Soldiers of the Plough.
       Kind heaven speed the Plough!
       And bless the hands that guide it;
         God gives the seed—
         The bread we need,
       Man's labour must provide it.

Blest is his lot, in hall or cot,
   Who lives as nature wills,
Who pours his corn from Ceres' horn,
   And quaffs his native rills!
No breeze that sweeps trade's stormy deeps,
   Can touch his golden prow;
Their foes are few, their lives are true,
   The Soldiers of the Plough.
      Kind heaven speed the Plough!
      And bless the hands that guide it;
       God gives the seed—
       The bread we need,
      Man's labour must provide it.

v.

Fast sped the rushing chariot of the Hours.
Without, the Harvest Moon, through fleecy bowers
Of hazy cloudlets, swept her graceful way,
Proud as an empress on her marriage-day;
The admiring planets lit her stately march
With smiles that gleamed along the silent arch,
And all the starry midnight blazed with light,
As if 'twere earth and heaven's nuptial-night;
The cock crowed, certain that the day had broke,
The aged house-dog suddenly awoke,
And bayed so loud a challenge to the moon,
From the old orchard fled the thievish 'coon:
Within, the lightest hearts that ever beat
Still found their harmless pleasures pure and sweet;
The fire still burned on the capacious hearth,
In sympathy with the redundant mirth;

Old graybeards felt the glow of youth revive,
Old matrons smiled upon the human hive,
Where life's rare nectar, fit for gods to sip,
In forfeit kisses passed from lip to lip.
Be hushed rude Mirth! as merry as the May
Is she who comes to sing her roundelay:

CLAIRE.

Whither now, blushing Claire?
Maid of the sylph-like air,
Blooming and debonair,
    Whither so early?
Chasing the merry morn,
Down through the golden corn?
List'ning the hunter's horn
    Ring through the barley?

" Flowerets fresh and fair,"
Answered the blushing Claire,
" Fit for my bridal hair,
    Bloom 'mongst the barley;
Hark! 'tis the hunter's horn,
Waking the sylvan morn,
And through the yellow corn
    Comes my brave Charlie."

Through the dew-dripping grain
Pressed the heart-stricken swain,
Crushed with a weight of pain,

Drooped like the barley;
Ah! timid shepherd boy!
Man's love should ne'er be coy,
Sweet is Claire's maiden joy,
Kissing her Charlie!

VI.

A pleasant soul as ever trilled a song
Was hers who warbled "Claire."   All the day long
Her voice was ringing like a bridal bell;
Gladness and joy leaped up at every swell;
And love was deeper, warmer, for the tone
That clasped the heart like an enchanted zone.
A youth was there more comely than the rest;
One who could turn a furrow with the best,
Compete for manly strength and portly air,
Or wield a scythe with any reaper there.
The spirit of her voice had moved above
The waters of his soul, and waked his song to Love:

BALLAD.

" Come tell me, merry Brooklet, of a gentle Maid I seek,
Thou'lt know her by the freshness of the rose upon her
        cheek;
Her eyes are chaste and tender, and so serenely bright,
You can read her heart's pure secrets by their warm
        religious light."

" The Maid has not come hither," said the Brooklet in
     reply ;
" I've listened for her footfall ere the stars were in the
     sky ;
The Fountain has been singing of a Maid, with eyes so
     bright
You may read the cherished secrets of her bosom by
     their light."

" Pray tell me, merry Brooklet, what saith her thoughts
     of one
Who wronged her loving nature ere the setting of the
     sun ?
What say they of yon autumn moon that smiles so
     mournfully
On the slowly-dying season, and the blasted moorland
     tree ?"

" She sitteth by the Fountain," the Brook replied again,
" Her heart as pure as heaven, and her thoughts without
     a stain ;
' Oh, fickle moon, and changeful man !' she saith, ' a year
     ago
All the paths were true-love-lighted where I'm groping
     now in woe.'

" She sitteth by the Fountain, the gentle mists arise,
And kiss away the tear-pearls that tremble in her eyes;
The Fountain singeth to me that the Maiden in her
     dream
Shrinks as the vapours claim her as the Oread of the
     stream."

Off sped the merry Streamlet adown the sloping vale ;
The Shepherd seeks the Fountain, where sits the
      Maiden pale;
And to the wandering Brooklet, through many a lonely
      wild,
The burden of the Fountain was, that Love was
      reconciled.

VII.

But soon the Morn, on many a distant height,
Fingers the raven locks of lingering Night ;
The last dark shadows that precede the day
Have stripped the splendour from the Milky Way ;
And Nature seems disturbed by fitful dreams,
As one who shudders when the owlet screams ;
The painful burden of the Whippoorwill,
Like a vague Sorrow, floats from hill to hill ;
Along the vales the doleful accents run,
Where the white vapours dread the burning sun ;
While human voices stir the haunted air,
One sings " the Plough," another warbles " Claire:"
The Happy Harvesters, a lightsome throng,
Dispersing homewards, prove the excellence of Song.

THE FALLS OF THE CHAUDIÈRE, OTTAWA.

I have laid my cheek to Nature's, placed my puny hand
    in hers,
    Felt a kindred spirit warming all the life-blood of my
        face,
Moved amid the very foremost of her truest worshippers,
    Studying each curve of beauty, marking every minute
        grace ;
Loved not less the mountain cedar than the flowers at
    its feet,
    Looking skyward from the valley, open-lipped as if in
        prayer,
Felt a pleasure in the brooklet singing of its wild
    retreat,
    But I knelt before the splendour of the thunderous
        Chaudière.

All my manhood waked within me, every nerve had
    tenfold force,
    And my soul stood up rejoicing, looking on with
        cheerful eyes,
Watching the resistless waters speeding on their down-
    ward course,
    Titan strength and queenly beauty diademed with
        rainbow dyes.
Eye and ear, with spirit quickened, mingled with the
    lovely strife,
    Saw the living Genius shrined within her sanctuary
        fair,

Heard her voice of sweetness singing, peered into her
    hidden life,
  And discerned the tuneful secret of the jubilant Chau-
      dière :

  " Within my pearl-roofed shell,
Whose floor is woven with the iris bright,
Genius and Queen of the Chaudière I dwell,
As in a world of immaterial light.

  My throne, an ancient rock,
Marked by the feet of ages long-departed,
My joy, the cataract's stupendous shock,
Whose roll is music to the grateful-hearted.

  I've seen the eras glide
With muffled tread to their eternal dreams,
While I have lived in vale and mountain side,
With leaping torrents and sweet purling streams.

  The Red-Man's active life ;
His love, pride, passions, courage, and great deeds ;
His perfect freedom, and his thirst for strife ;
His swift revenge, at which the memory bleeds :

  The sanguinary years,
When sullen Terror, like a raging Fate,
Swept down the stately tribes like slaughtered deers,
And war and hatred joined to decimate

  The remnants of the race,
And spread decay through centuries of pain—
No more I mark their sure, avenging pace,
And forests wave where war-whoops shook the plain.

Their deeds I envied not.
The royal tyrant on his purple throne,
I, in secluded grove or shady grot,
Had purer joys than he had ever known.

God made the ancient hills,
The valleys and the solemn wildernesses,
The merry-hearted and melodious rills,
And strung with diamond dews the pine-trees' tresses ;

But man's hand built the palace,
And he that reigns therein is simply man ;
Man turns God's gifts to poison in the chalice
That brimmed with nectar in the primal plan.

Here I abide alone—
The wild Chaudière's eternal jubilee
Has such sweet divination in its tone,
And utters nature's truest prophecy

In thunderings of zeal !
I've seen the Atheist in terror start,
Awed to contrition by the strong appeal
That waked conviction in his doubting heart :

    ' Teachers speak throughout all nature,
       From the womb of Silence born,
    Heed ye not their words, O Scoffer ?
       Flinging back thy scorn with scorn !
    To the desert spring that leapeth,
       Pulsing, from the parchèd sod,
    Points the famished trav'ler, saying—
       ' Brothers, here, indeed, is God !'

From the patriarchal fountains,
   Sending forth their tribes of rills,
From the cedar-shadowed lakelets
   In the hearts of distant hills,
Whispers softer than the moonbeams
   Wisdom's gentle heart have awed,
Till its lips approved the cadence—
   'Surely here, indeed, is God!'

Lo! o'er all, the Torrent Prophet,
   An inspired Demosthenes,
To the Doubter's soul appealing,
   Louder than the preacher-seas:
Dreamer! wouldst have nature spurn thee
   For a dumb, insensate clod?
Dare to doubt! and these shall teach thee
   Of a truth there lives a God!'

By day and night, for hours,
I watch the cataract's impulsive leap,
Refreshed and gladdened by the cheering showers
Wrung from the passion of the seething deep.

Pleased when the buried waves
Emerge again, like incorporeal hosts
Rising, white-sheeted, from their gloomy graves,
As if the depths had yielded up their ghosts.

And when the midnight storm
Enfolds the welkin in its robe of clouds,
Through the dim vapours of the cauldron swarm
The sheeted spectres in their whitest shrouds,

By the lightning's flash betrayed.
These gather from the insubstantial vapour
The lunar rainbows, which by them are made—
Woven with moonbeams by some starry taper,

To decorate the halls
Of my fair palace, whence I'm pained to see
Thy human brethren watch the waterfalls—
Not with such rev'rence as I've found in thee:

Too many with an eye
To speculation and the worldling's dreams;
Others, who seek from nature no reply,
Nor read the oral language of the streams.

But of the few who loved
The beautiful with grateful heart and soul,
Who looked on nature fondly, and were moved
By one sweet glance, as by the mighty whole:

Of these, the thoughtful few,
Thou wert the first to seek the inner temple,
And stand before the Priestess. Thou wert true
To nature and thyself. Be thy example

The harbinger of times
When the Chaudière's imposing majesty
Will awe the spirits of the heartless mimes
To worship God in truth, with nature's constancy."

Still I heard the mellow sweetness of her voice at inter-
    vals,
    Mingling with the fall of waters, rising with the
        snowy spray,
Ringing through the sportive current like the joy of
    waterfalls,
    Sending up their hearty vespers at the calmy close of
        day.
'Loath to leave the scene of beauty, lover-like I stayed,
    and stayed,
    Folding to my eager bosom memories beyond com-
        pare ;
Deeper, stronger, more enduring than my dreams of wood
    and glade,
    Were the eloquent appeals of the magnificent Chau-
        dière.

E'en the solid bridge is trembling, whence I look my
    last farewell,
    Dizzy with the roar and trampling of the mighty
        herd of waves,
Speeding past the rocky Island, steadfast as a sentinel,
    Towards the loveliest bay that ever mirrored the
        Algonquin Braves.
Soul of Beauty ! Genius ! Spirit ! Priestess of the lovely
    strife !
    In my heart thy words are shrined, as in a sanctuary
        fair ;
Echoes of thy voice of sweetness, rousing all my better
    life,
    Ever haunt my wildest visions of the jubilant Chau-
        dière.

A ROYAL WELCOME.

By England's side we stand,
We grasp her royal hand,
And pay her rightful homage through her Son;
Thank God for England's care!
Thank God for Britain's heir!
Our hearts go forth to meet him—we are one.

A loyal Province pours
Her thousands to her shores,
From iron-girt Superior to the sea;
We feel our youthful blood
Surge through us like a flood,
There's not a slave amongst us—we are free.

For none but Freemen know
The truly loyal throe
That gives heroic impulse to the Man—
The passion and the fire,
The chivalrous desire:
Our Fathers all were heroes—in the van.

And we, their ardent sons,
Through whom, triumphant, runs
The old intrepid attribute serene,
Would leave our chosen land,
Our homes, our forests grand,
To strike for England's honour and her Queen.

No soulless welcome we
Dare give to such as thee:
Be thou a bright example to the world;
Great in thy well-earned fame,
Beloved in heart and name,
Wherever Britain's banner is unfurled.

Through all our leafy glades,
Through all our green arcades,
The living torrents, sweeping in, evince
That from their manly hearts
The Yeoman chorus starts:
' Honour to England's Heir!—long live the Prince!'

Oh, England! in this hour
We own thy sov'reign pow'r;
To thee and thine our best affections cling;
And when thy crown is laid
On Royal Albert's head,
With heart and soul we'll shout—GOD SAVE THE
KING!

MALCOLM.   61

MALCOLM.

Boy! this world has ever been
  A bright, glad world to me;
Through each dark and checkered scene
  God's sun shone lovingly.
But Content I've never known;
  Hoping, trusting that the years,
  With their April smiles and tears,
  Would yet bring me one like thee
      That I could call my own.

With thy soft and heavenly eyes
  In deep and pensive calm,
I seem looking at the skies,
  And wonder where I am!
Something more than princely blood
  Courses in thy tranquil face:
  When she lent thee such a grace,
  Nature lit life's earnest flame
      In her most queenly mood.

Such a sweet intelligence
  Is stamped on every line,
Banqueting our craving sense
  With minist'rings divine.
If thy Boyhood be so great,
  What will be the coming Man,
  Could we overleap the span?
  Are there treasures in the mine,
      To pay us, if we wait?

Doth the voice of Music live
  In that majestic brain,
Waiting for the Hand to give
  Expression to the strain ?
Are there wells of Truth—pure, deep,
  Where the patient diver, Thought,
  Finds the pearl that has been sought
Many a weary age in vain,
    Entrusted to thy keep.

Doth the fire of Genius burn
  Within that ample brow ?
Or some patient spirit yearn
  For things that are not now ?
Hidden in the over-soul
  Of the Future, to be born
  When the world has ceased its scorn,
When the sceptic's heart will bow
    To the divine control.

Patiently we'll watch and hope,
  And wait, alternately ;
Trusting that, when time shall ope
  The casket's mystery,
We will be made rich indeed
  With the wonders it contains ;
Rich beyond all previous gains ;
  Richer for thy thought and thee,
    Beyond our greatest meed.

THE COMET—OCTOBER, 1858.

Erratic Soul of some great Purpose, doomed
To track the wild illimitable space,
Till sure propitiation has been made
For the divine commission unperformed !
What was thy crime ? Ahasuerus' curse
Were not more stern on earth than thine in Heaven !

Art thou the Spirit of some Angel World,
For grave rebellion banished from thy peers,
Compelled to watch the calm, immortal stars,
Circling in rapture the celestial void,
While the avenger follows in thy train
To spur thee on to wretchedness eterne ?

Or one of nature's wildest fantasies,
From which she flies in terror so profound,
And with such whirl of torment in her breast,
That mighty earthquakes yearn where'er she treads ;
While War makes red its terrible right hand,
And Famine stalks abroad all lean and wan ?

To us thou art as exquisitely fair
As the ideal visions of the seer,
Or gentlest fancy that e'er floated down
Imagination's bright, unruffled stream,
Wedding the thought that was too deep for words
To the low breathings of inspirèd song.

When the stars sang together o'er the birth
Of the poor Babe at Bethlehem, that lay
In the coarse manger at the crowded Inn,
Didst thou, perhaps a bright exalted star,
Refuse to swell the grand, harmonious lay,
Jealous as Herod of the birth divine ?

Or when the crown of thorns on Calvary
Pierced the Redeemer's brow, didst thou disdain
To weep, when all the planetary worlds
Were blinded by the fulness of their tears ?
E'en to the flaming sun, that hid his face
At the loud cry, " Lama Sabachthani !"

No rest !   No rest ! the very damned have that
In the dark councils of remotest Hell,
Where the dread scheme was perfected that sealed
Thy disobedience and accruing doom.
Like Adam's sons, hast thou, too, forfeited
The blest repose that never pillowed Sin ?

No ! none can tell thy fate, thou wandering
        Sphinx !
Pale Science, searching by the midnight lamp
Through the vexed mazes of the human brain,
Still fails to read the secret of its soul
As the superb enigma flashes by,
A loosed Prometheus burning with disdain.

AUTUMN.

If seasons, like the human race, had souls,
Then two artistic spirits live within
The Chameleon mind of Autumn—these,
The Poet's mentor and the Painter's guide.
The myriad-thoughted phases of the mind
Are truly represented by the hues
That thrill the forests with prophetic fire.
And what could painter's skill compared to these?
What palette ever held the flaming tints
That on these leafy hieroglyphs foretell
How set the ebbing currents of the year?
What poet's page was ever like to this,
Or told the lesson of life's waning days
More forcibly, with more of natural truth,
Than yon red maples, or these poplars, white
As the pale shroud that wraps some human corse?
And then, again, the spirit of a King,
Clothed with that majesty most monarchs lack,
Might fit old Autumn for his royal rule:
For here is kingly ermine, cloth of gold,
And purple robes well worthy to be worn
By the best monarch that e'er donned a crown.

Proclaim him Royal Autumn! Poet King!
The Laureate of the Seasons, whose rare songs
Are such as lyrist never hoped to fling
On the fine ear of an admiring world.
Autumn, the Poet, Painter, and true King!
His gorgeous Ideality speaks forth

E

From the rare colors of the changing leaves;
And the ripe blood that swells his purple veins
Is as the glowing of a sacred fire.
He walks with Shelley's spirit on the cliffs
Of the Ethereal Caucasus, and o'er
The summits of the Euganean hills;
And meets the soul of Wordsworth, in profound
And philosophic meditation, rapt
In some great dream of love towards
The human race.   The cheery Spring may come,
And touch the dreaming flowers into life,
Summer expand her leafy sea of green,
And wake the joyful wilderness to song,
As a fair hand strikes music from a lyre:
But Autumn, from its daybreak to its close,
Setting in florid beauty, like the sun,
Robed with rare brightness and ethereal flame,
Holds all the year's ripe fruitage in its hands,
And dies with songs of praise upon its lips.

And then, the Indian Summer, bland as June:
Some Tuscarora King, Algonquin Seer,
Or Huron Chief, returned to smoke the Pipe
Of Peace upon the ancient hunting grounds;
The mighty shade in spirit walking forth
To feel the beauty of his native woods,
Flashing in Autumn vestures, or to mark
The scanty remnants of the scattered tribes
Wending towards their graves.   Few Braves are left;
Few mighty Hunters; fewer stately Chiefs,
Like great Tecumseth fit to take the field,
And lead the tribes to certain victory,

Choosing annihilation to defeat :
But having run the gauntlet of their days,
This Autumn remnant of some unknown race,
Nearing the Winter of their sad decay,
Fall like dry leaves into the lap of Time ;
Their old trunks sapless, their tough branches bare,
And Fate's shrill war-whoop thund'ring at their heels.

COLIN.

Who'll dive for the dead men now,
 Since Colin is gone?
Who'll feel for the anguished brow,
 Since Colin is gone?
True Feeling is not confined
To the learned or lordly mind;
Nor can it be bought and sold
In exchange for an Alp of gold;
For Nature, that never lies,
Flings back with indignant scorn
The counterfeit deed, still-born,
In the face of the seeming wise,
In the Janus face of the huckster race
Who barter her truths for lies.

Who'll wrestle with dangers dire,
 Since Colin is gone?
Who'll fearlessly brave the maniac wave,
Thoughtless of self, human life to save,
Unmoved by the storm-fiend's ire?
Who, Shadrach-like, will walk through fire,
 Since Colin is gone?
Or hang his life on so frail a breath
That there's but a step 'twixt life and death?
For Courage is not the heritage
Of the nobly born; and many a sage
Has climbed to the temple of fame,
And written his deathless name
In letters of golden flame,
Who, on glancing down

From his high renown,
Saw his unlettered sire
Still by the old log fire,
Saw the unpolished dame—
And the dunghill from which he came.

Ah, ye who judge the dead
By the outward lives they led,
And not by the hidden worth
Which none but God can see;
Ye who would spurn the earth
That covers such as he;
Would ye but bare your hearts,
Cease to play borrowed parts,
And come down from your self-built throne:
How few from their house of glass,
As the gibbering secrets pass,
Would dare to fling, whether serf or king,
The first accusing stone!

Peace, peace to his harmless dust!
　　Since Colin is gone;
We can but hope and trust;
.Man judgeth, but God is just;
　　Poor Colin is gone!
Had he faults?　His heart was true,
And warm as the summer's sun.
Had he failings?　Ay, but few;
'Twas an honest race he run.
Let him rest in the poor man's grave,
Ye who grant him no higher goal;
There may be a curse on the hands that gave,
But not on his simple soul!

MARGERY.

" Truth lights our minds as sunrise lights the world.
The heart that shuts out truth, excludes the light
That wakes the love of beauty in the soul;
And being foe to these, despises God,
The sole Dispenser of the gracious bliss
That brings us nearer the celestial gate.
They who might feed on rose-leaves of the True,
And grow in loveliness of heart and soul,
Catch at Deception's airy gossamers,
As children clutch at stars.   To some, the world
Is a bleak desert, parched with blinding sand,
With here and there a mirage, fair to view,
But insubstantial as the visions born
Of Folly and Despair.   Could we but know
How nigh we are to the true light of heaven;
In what a world of love we live and breathe;
On what a tide of truth our souls are borne!
Yet we're but bubbles in the whirl of life,
Mere flecks upon its ever-restless sea,
Meteors in its ever-changing sky.
Eternity alone is worth the thought
That we expend upon the passing hour,
Chasing the gaudy butterflies that lure
Our footsteps from the path that leads us home.
We will not see the beacon on the rock;
The prompter is unheeded; and the spark
Of the true spirit quenched in utter night,
As we rush headlong, wrecked on Error's shoals.
Some hearts will never open; all their wards

Have grown so rusty, that the golden key
Of Love Divine must fail to move the bolt
That Self has drawn to keep God's angels out."

So spake the merry Margery, the while
Her fingers lengthened out a filigree,
That seemed to me so many golden threads
Of thought between her fingers and her brain,
Bestrung with priceless pearls; her lightsome mood,
Worn as occasion might necessitate,
Replaced to-night by sober-sided Sense,
That made her beauty like an eve in June,
Just as the moon is risen.   I, to mark
My approbation of her present mood,
Rehearsed a rambling lyric of my own,
That seemed prophetic of her thoughts to-night :

    Within my mind there ever lives
       A yearning for the True,
    The Beautiful and Good.   God gives
       These, as He gives the dew

    That falls upon the flowers at night,
       The grass, the thirsty trees,
    Because 'tis needful; and the light
       That suns my mind from these—

    Truth—Beauty—Goodness, doth but fill
       A void within my soul ;
    And I fall prone before the Will
       Of Him who gave the whole—

The wondrous life—the power to think,
  And love, and act, and speak.
Standing, half-poised, upon the brink
  Of being—strong, yet weak—

Strong in vast hopes, but weak in deeds,
  I lift my heart and pray,
That where the tangled skein of creeds
  Excludes the light of day

From human minds, God's purposes
  May be made plain, that all
May walk in truth's and wisdom's ways,
  And lay aside the thrall

Of enmity, whose clouds have kept
  Their souls as dark as night;
That they whose love and hope have slept,
  May come into the light,

And live as men, with minds to grasp
  Within the sphere of thought
The boundless universe, and clasp
  The good the wise have sought,

As if it were a long-lost dove,
  Or a stray soul returned
To worship in the fane of love,
  That it so long had spurned.

Where'er I gaze, my eyes behold
  Nought but the beautiful.
The world is grand as it is old;
  The only fitting school

For man, where he may learn to live,
   And live to learn that what
He needs heaven will in mercy give.
   Whatever be his lot,

He shapes it for himself; his mind
   Is his own heaven or hell:
Just as he peoples it, he'll find
   Himself compelled to dwell

With good or evil.   Good abounds
   In this delightful sphere;
But man will walk his daily rounds,
   And evermore give ear

To the false promptings that waylay
   His steps at every turn;
Flinging the true and good away
   For joys that he should spurn,

As being all unworthy of
   His greatness as a man.
Why, man!—why tremble at the scoff
   Of fools and bigots?   Scan

The mental firmament, and see
   How men in every age,
Who strove for immortality—
   Whose errand was to wage

Not War, but Peace—men of pure minds,
   Who sought and found the truth,
And treasured it, as one who finds
   The secret of lost Youth

Restored and made immortal—see
  How they were scorned, because
Their Sphinx-lives spake of mystery
  To those to whom the laws

Of nature are as claspèd books!—
  Poets, who ruled the world
Of Thought; in whose prophetic looks
  And minds there lay impearled,

But hidden from the vulgar sight,
  Such universal truths,
That many, blinded by the light—
  Gray-haired, green-gosling youths,

With whips of satire, looks of scorn,
  And finger of disdain,
Have crushed these harbingers of morn,
  But could not kill the strain

That was a part of nature's mind,
  And therefore can not die.
That which men spurned, angels have shrined
  Among God's truths on high.

And so 't will ever be, till man
  Knows more of Goodness, Truth,
And Beauty—more of nature's plan,
  And Love that brings back youth

To hearts that have grown frail and old
  By groping in the dark
With blinded eyes; their idol, Gold,
  And Gain, their Pleasure-bark!

" 'Tis well that nature hath her ministers,"
She said, her voice and looks so passing sweet ;
" Great-hearts that let in love, and keep it there,
Like the true flame within the diamond's heart,
Informing, blessing, chastening their lives.
Man has but one great love—his love for God ;
All other loves are lesser and more less
As they recede from Him, as are the streams
The farthest from the fountain.   God is Love.
Who loves God most, loves most his fellow-men ;
Sees the Creator in the creature's form
Where others see but man—and he, so frail
The very devils are akin to him !
There is no light that is not born of love ;
No truth where love is not its guiding star ;
Faith without love is noonday without sun,
For love begetteth works both good and true,
And these give faith its immortality."

We parted at the outer door.   The stars
Seemed never half so bright or numberless
As they appeared to-night.   Margery's laugh
Tripped after me in merry cadences,
Like the quick steps of fairies in the air
United to the chorus of their hearts
Breathed into silvery music.   Happy soul !
Nature's epitome in all her moods.

EVA.

" God bless the darling Eva !" was my prayer.
A pure, unconscious depth of earnestness
Was in her eyes, so indescribable
You might as well the color of the air
Seek to daguerreotype, or to impress
A stain upon the river, whose first swell
Would swirl it to the deep.   A calm, sweet soul,
Where Love's celestial saints and ministers
Did hold the earthly under such control
Virtue sprung up like daisies from the sod.
Oh, for one hour's sweet excellence like hers !
One hour of sinlessness, that never more
Can visit me this side the Silent Shore,
To stand, like her, serene, unblushing before God !

THE POET'S RECOMPENSE.

His heart's a burning censer, filled with spice
From fairer vales than those of Araby,
Breathing such prayers to heaven, that the nice
Discriminating ear of Deity
Can cull sweet praises from the rare perfume.
Man cannot know what starry lights illume
The soaring spirit of his brother man !
He judges harshly with his mind's eyes closed;
His loftiest understanding cannot scan
The heights where Poet-souls have oft reposed;
He cannot feel the chastened influence
Divine, that lights the Ideal atmosphere,
And never to his uninspirèd sense
Rolls the majestic hymn that inspirates the Seer.

THE WINE OF SONG.

Within Fancy's Halls I sit, and quaff
  Rich draughts of the Wine of Song;
    And I drink, and drink,
    To the very brink
  Of delirium wild and strong,
Till I lose all sense of the outer world,
  And see not the human throng.

The lyral chords of each rising thought
  Are swept by a hand unseen;
    And I glide, and glide,
    With my music bride,
  Where few spiritless souls have been;
And I soar afar on wings of sound,
  With my fair Æolian Queen.

Deep, deeper still, from the springs of Thought
  I quaff, till the fount is dry;
    And I climb, and climb,
    To a height sublime,
  Up the stars of some lyric sky,
Where I seem to rise upon airs that melt
  Into song as they pass by.

Millennial rounds of bliss I live,
  Withdrawn from my cumbrous clay,
    As I sweep, and sweep,
    Through infinite deep
  On deep of that starry spray;
Myself a sound on its world-wide round,
  A tone on its spheral way.

And wheresoe'er through the wondrous space
  My soul wings its noiseless flight,
    On their astral rounds
    Float divinest sounds,
  Unseen, save by spirit-sight,
Obeying some wise, eternal law,
  As fixed as the law of light.

But, oh, when my cup of dainty bliss
  Is drained of the Wine of Song,
    How I fall, and fall,
    At the sober call
  Of the body, that waiteth long
To hurry me back to its cares terrene,
  And earth's spiritless human throng.

THE PLAINS OF ABRAHAM.

I stood upon the Plain,
That had trembled when the slain,
Hurled their proud, defiant curses at the battle-heated
    foe,
When the steed dashed right and left,
Through the bloody gaps he cleft,
When the bridle-rein was broken, and the rider was
    laid low.

What busy feet had trod
Upon the very sod
Where I marshalled the battalions of my fancy to my
    aid!
And I saw the combat dire,
Heard the quick, incessant fire,
And the cannons' echoes startling the reverberating
    glade.

I saw them, one and all,
The banners of the Gaul
In the thickest of the contest, round the resolute Mont-
    calm;
The well-attended Wolfe,
Emerging from the gulf
Of the battle's fiery furnace, like the swelling of a
    psalm.

I heard the chorus dire,
That jarred along the lyre
On which the hymn of battle rung, like surgings of the
    wave
When the storm, at blackest night,
Wakes the ocean in affright,
As it shouts its mighty pibroch o'er some shipwrecked
    vessel's grave.

I saw the broad claymore
Flash from its scabbard, o'er
The ranks that quailed and shuddered at the close and
    fierce attack;
When Victory gave the word,
Then Scotland drew the sword,
And with arm that never faltered drove the brave de-
    fenders back.

I saw two great chiefs die,
Their last breaths like the sigh
Of the zephyr-sprite that wantons on the rosy lips of
    morn;
No envy-poisoned darts,
No rancour, in their hearts,
To unfit them for their triumph over death's impending
    scorn.

And as I thought and gazed,
My soul, exultant, praised
The Power to whom each mighty act and victory are
    due,

For the saint-like Peace that smiled
Like a heaven-gifted child,
And for the air of quietude that steeped the distant
view.

The sun looked down with pride,
And scattered far and wide
His beams of whitest glory till they flooded all the
Plain;
The hills their veils withdrew,
Of white, and purplish blue,
And reposed all green and smiling 'neath the shower of
golden rain.

Oh, rare, divinest life
Of Peace, compared with Strife!
Yours is the truest splendour, and the most enduring
fame;
All the glory ever reaped
Where the fiends of battle leaped,
Is harsh discord to the music of your undertoned
acclaim.

DEATH OF WOLFE.

"They run ! they run !"—"Who run ?"   Not they
    Who faced that decimating fire
    As coolly as if human ire
      Were rooted from their hearts ;
They run, while he who led the way
So bravely on that glorious day,
    Burns for one word with keen desire
      Ere waning life departs !

"They run ! they run !"—" *Who* run ?" he cried,
    As swiftly to his pallid brow,
    Like crimson sunlight upon snow,
      The anxious blood returned ;
" The French ! the French !" a voice replied,
When quickly paled life's ebbing tide,
    And though his words were weak and low
      His eye with valour burned.

" Thank God ! I die in peace," he said ;
    And calmly yielding up his breath,
    There trod the shadowy realms of death
      A good man and a brave ;
Through all the regions of the dead,
Behold his spirit, spectre-led,
    Crowned with the amaranthine wreath
      That blooms not for the slave.

BROCK.

OCTOBER 13TH, 1859.*

One voice, one people, one in heart
    And soul, and feeling, and desire !
    Re-light the smouldering martial fire,
    Sound the mute trumpet, strike the lyre,
    The hero deed can not expire,
        The dead still play their part.

Raise high the monumental stone !
    A nation's fealty is theirs,
    And we are the rejoicing heirs,
    The honored sons of sires whose cares
    We take upon us unawares,
        As freely as our own.

We boast not of the victory,
    But render homage, deep and just,
    To his—to their—immortal dust,
    Who proved so worthy of their trust
    No lofty pile nor sculptured bust
        Can herald their degree.

No tongue need blazon forth their fame—
    The cheers that stir the sacred hill
    Are but mere promptings of the will
    That conquered then, that conquers still;
    And generations yet shall thrill
        At Brock's remembered name.

* The day of the inauguration of the new Monument on Queenston Heights.

Some souls are the Hesperides
　　Heaven sends to guard the golden age,
　　Illuming the historic page
　　With records of their pilgrimage;
　　True Martyr, Hero, Poet, Sage:
　　　And he was one of these.

Each in his lofty sphere sublime
　　Sits crowned above the common throng,
　　Wrestling with some Pythonic wrong,
　　In prayer, in thunder, thought, or song;
　　Briareus-limbed, they sweep along,
　　　The Typhons of the time.

SONG FOR CANADA.

Sons of the race whose sires
Aroused the martial flame
    That filled with smiles
    The triune Isles,
Through all their heights of fame!
With hearts as brave as theirs,
With hopes as strong and high,
    We'll ne'er disgrace
    The honoured race
Whose deeds can never die.   .
    Let but the rash intruder dare
      To touch our darling strand,
        The martial fires
        That thrilled our sires
      Would flame throughout the land.

Our lakes are deep and wide,
Our fields and forests broad;
    With cheerful air
    We'll speed the share,
And break the fruitful sod;
Till blest with rural peace,
Proud of our rustic toil,
    On hill and plain
    True kings we'll reign,
The victors of the soil.
    But let the rash intruder dare

To touch our darling strand,
 The martial fires
 That thrilled our sires
Would light him from the land.

Health smiles with rosy face
Amid our sunny dales,
 And torrents strong
 Fling hymn and song
Through all the mossy vales;
Our sons are living men,
Our daughters fond and fair;
 A thousand isles
 Where Plenty smiles,
Make glad the brow of Care.
 But let the rash intruder dare
 To touch our darling strand,
 The martial fires
 That thrilled our sires
 Would flame throughout the land.

And if in future years
One wretch should turn and fly,
 Let weeping Fame
 Blot out his name
From Freedom's hallowed sky;
Or should our sons e'er prove
A coward, traitor race,—
 Just heaven! frown
 In thunder down,
T' avenge the foul disgrace!

But let the rash intruder dare
To touch our darling strand,
The martial fires
That thrilled our sires
Would light him from the land.

SONG.—I'D BE A FAIRY KING.

Oh, I'd be a Fairy King,
  With my vassals brave and bold;
    We'd hunt all day,
    Through the wildwood gay,
  In our guise of green and gold;
And we'd lead such a merry, merry life,
  That the silly, toiling bee,
    Would have no sweet
    In its dull retreat,
So rich as our frolic glee.
    I'd be a Fairy King,
      With my vassals brave and bold;
        We'd hunt all day,
        Through the wildwood gay,
      In our guise of green and gold.

At night, when the moon spake down,
  With her bland and pensive tone,
    The fairest Queen
    That ever was seen
  Would sit on my pearly throne;
And we'd lead such a merry, merry life,
  That the stars would laugh in show'rs
    Of silver light,
    All the summer night,
To the airs of the passing Hours.
    I'd be a Fairy King,
      With my vassals brave and bold;
        We'd hunt all day
        Through the wildwood gay,
      In our guise of green and gold.

We'd talk with the dainty flow'rs,
  And we'd chase the laughing brooks ;
    My merry men,
    Through grove and glen,
  Would search for the mossy nooks ;
And we'd be such a merry, merry band,
  Such a lively-hearted throng,
    That life would seem
    But a silvery dream
In the flowery Land of Song.
    I'd be a Fairy King,
      With my vassals brave and bold ;
      We'd hunt all day,
      Through the wildwood gay,
    In our guise of green and gold.

SONG.—LOVE WHILE YOU MAY.

Day by day, with startling fleetness,
    Life speeds away ;
Love, alone, can glean its sweetness,
    Love while you may.
While the soul is strong and fearless,
While the eye is bright and tearless,
Ere the heart is chilled and cheerless—
    Love while you may.

Life may pass, but love, undying,
    Dreads no decay ;
Even from the grave replying,
    " Love while you may."
Love's the fruit, as life's the flower ;
Love is heaven's rarest dower ;
Love gives love its quick'ning power—
    Love while you may.

THE SNOWS.

UPPER OTTAWA.

Over the snows,
Buoyantly goes
The lumberers' bark canoe;
Lightly they sweep,
Wilder each leap,
Rending the white caps through.
Away! away!
With the speed of a startled deer,
While the steersman true,
And his laughing crew,
Sing of their wild career:

"Mariners glide
Far o'er the tide,
In ships that are staunch and strong;
Safely as they,
Speed we away,
Waking the woods with song."
Away! away!
With the flight of a startled deer,
While the laughing crew
Of the swift canoe
Sing of the raftsmen's cheer:

"Through forest and brake,
O'er rapid and lake,
We're sport for the sun and rain;
Free as the child
Of the Arab wild,
Hardened to toil and pain.

Away! away!
With the speed of a startled deer,
　While our buoyant flight,
　And the rapid's might,
Heighten our swift career."

　Over the snows
　Buoyantly goes
The lumberers' bark canoe;
　Lightly they sweep,
　Wilder each leap,
Tearing the white caps through.
　Away! away!
With the speed of a startled deer;
　There's a fearless crew
　In each light canoe,
To sing of the raftsmen's cheer.

THE RAPID.

ST. LAWRENCE.

All peacefully gliding,
The waters dividing,
The indolent bátteau moved slowly along,
The rowers, light-hearted,
From sorrow long parted,
Beguiled the dull moments with laughter and song:
"Hurrah for the Rapid! that merrily, merrily
Gambols and leaps on its tortuous way;
Soon we will enter it, cheerily, cheerily,
Pleased with its freshness, and wet with its spray."

More swiftly careering,
The wild Rapid nearing,
They dash down the stream like a terrified steed;
The surges delight them,
No terrors affright them,
Their voices keep pace with their quickening speed:
"Hurrah for the Rapid! that merrily, merrily
Shivers its arrows against us in play;
Now we have entered it, cheerily, cheerily,
Our spirits as light as its feathery spray.'

Fast downward they're dashing,
Each fearless eye flashing,
Though danger awaits them on every side;
Yon rock—see it frowning!
They strike—they are drowning!
But downward they speed with the merciless tide:

No voice cheers the Rapid, that angrily, angrily
Shivers their bark in its maddening play;
Gaily they entered it—heedlessly recklessly,
Mingling their lives with its treacherous spray!

LOST AND FOUND.

In the mildest, greenest grove
  . Blest by sprite or fairy,
Where the melting echoes rove,
  Voices sweet and airy ;
      Where the streams
      Drink the beams
      Of the Sun,
      As they run
      Riverward
      Through the sward,
A shepherd went astray—
E'en gods have lost their way.

Every bird had sought its nest,
  And each flower-spirit
Dreamed of that delicious rest
  Mortals ne'er inherit ;
      Through the trees
      Swept the breeze,
      Bringing airs
      Unawares
      Through the grove,
      Until love
Came down upon his heart,
Refusing to depart.

Hungrily he quaffed the strain,
  Sweeter still, and clearer,
Drenched with music's mellow rain,
  Nearer—nearer—dearer !

Chains of sound
Gently bound
The lost Youth,
Till, in sooth,
He stood there
A prisoner,
Raised between earth and heaven
By love's divinest leaven.

Was there ever such a face?
  Was it not a vision?
Had he climbed the starry space,
  To the fields Elysian?
        Through the glade
        The milk-maid
        With her pail,
        To the vale
        Passed along,
        Breathing song
Through all his ravished sense,
To gladden his suspense.

"Love is swift as hawk or hind,
  Chamois-like in fleetness,
None are lost that love can find,"
  Sang the maid, with sweetness.
        "True, in sooth,"
        Thought the Youth,
        "Strong, as swift,
        Love can lift

G

Mountain weights
To the gates
Of the celestial skies,
Where all else fades and dies."

Lightly flew the sunny days,
Joy and gladness sending;
Life becomes a song of praise
When true hearts are blending.
Guileless truth
Won the Youth,
Kept him there,
A prisoner;
While dear Love
From above
Poured down enduring dreams,
In calm supernal gleams.

YOUNG AGAIN.

Young again! Young again!
 Beating heart! I deemed that sorrow,
With its torture-rack of pain,
 Had eclipsed each bright to-morrow;
 And that Love could never rise
 Into life's cerulean skies,
 Singing the divine refrain—
  "Young again! Young again!"

Young again! Young again!
 Passion dies as we grow older;
Love that in repose has lain,
 Takes a higher flight, and bolder:
 Fresh from rest and dewy sleep,
 Like the skylark's matin sweep,
 Singing the divine refrain—
  "Young again! Young again!"

Young again! Young again!
 Book of Youth, thy sunny pages
Here and there a tear may stain,
 But 'tis Love that makes us sages.
 Love, Hope, Youth—blest trinity!
 Wanting these, and what were we?
 Who would chant the sweet refrain—
  "Young again! Young again!"

GLIMPSES.

Sounds of rural life and labour!
Not the notes of pipe and tabour,
Not the clash of helm and sabre
  Bright'ning up the field of glory,
Can compare with thy ovations,
That make glad the hearts of nations;
E'en the poet's fond creations
  Pale before thy simple story.

In the years beyond our present,
King was little more than peasant,
Labour was the shining crescent,
  Toil, the poor man's crown of glory;
Have we passed from worse to better
Since we wove the silken fetter,
Changed the plough for book and letter.
  Truest life for tinsel story?

Up the ladder of the ages
Clomb the patriarchal sages,
Solving nature's secret pages,
  Kings of thought's supremest glory;
Eagle-winged, and sight far reaching—
Are we wiser for their teaching?—
Wrangling creeds for gentle preaching!
  Falsest life for truest story!

Man is overfraught with culture,
Virtue early finds sepúlture,
While our vices sate the vulture

We misname a bird of glory;
Life is blindly artificial,
Rarely pass we its initial,
All our aims are prejudicial
    To its earnest, simple story.

Hail, primeval life and labour!
Martial notes of pipe and tabour,
Gleam of spears and clash of sabre,
    Hero march from fields of glory,
All the thundering ovations
Surging from the hearts of nations,
Poet dreams and speculations,
    Pale before thy simple story!

MY PRAYER.

O God! forgive the erring thought,
  The erring word and deed,
And in thy mercy hear the Christ
  Who comes to intercede.

My sins, like mountain-weights of lead,
  Weigh heavy on my soul;
I'm bruised and broken in this strife,
  But Thou canst make me whole.

Allay this fever of unrest,
  That fights against the Will;
And in Thy still small voice do Thou
  But whisper, " Peace, be still!"

Until within this heart of mine
  Thy lasting peace come down,
Will all the waves of Passion roll,
  Each good resolve to drown.

We walk in blindness and dark night
  Through half our earthly way;
Our clouds of weaknesses obscure
  The glory of the day.

We cannot lead the lives we would,
  But grope in dumb amaze,
Leaving the straight and flowery paths
  To tread the crooked ways.

We are as pilgrims toiling on
  Through all the weary hours;
And our poor hands are torn with thorns,
  Plucking life's tempting flowers.

We worship at a thousand shrines,
  And build upon the sands,
Passing the one great Temple, and
  The Rock on which it stands.

O, fading dream of human life!
  What can this change portend?
I long for higher walks, and true
  Progression without end.

Here I know nothing, and my search
  Can find no secret out;
I cannot think a single thought
  That is not mixed with doubt.

Relying on the higher source,
  The influence divine,   .
I can but hope that light may dawn
  Within this soul of mine.

I ask not wisdom, such as that
  To which the world is prone,
Nor knowledge ask, unless it come
  Direct from God alone.

Send down then, God! in mercy send
  Thy Love and Truth to me,
That I may henceforth walk in ligh'
  That comes direct from Thee.

HER STAR.

When the heavens throb and vibrate
　All along their silver veins,
To the mellow storm of music
　Sweeping o'er the starry trains,
Heard by few, as erst by shepherds
　On the far Chaldean plains:

Not the blazing, torch-like planets,
　Not the Pleiads wild and free,
Not Arcturus, Mars, Uranus,
　Bring the brightest dreams to me;
But I gaze in rapt devotion
　On the central star of three.

Central star of three that tingle
　In the balmy southern sky;
One above, and one below it,
　Dreamily they pale and die,
As two lesser minds might dwindle,
　When some great soul, passing by,

Stops, and reads their cherished secrets,
　With a calm and godlike air,
Luring all their radiance from them
　Leaving a dim twilight there,
Something vague, and half unreal,
　Like the Alpha of despair.

Gazing thus, and holding converse
    With the silence of my heart,
I would speak with famed Orion,
    I would question it apart,
Wrest her love's strange secret from it,
    If there's strength in human art.

And there come to me sweet whispers,
    Half in answer, half in thought :—
" Be but strong, impassioned mortal !
    Love will come to thee unsought;
Love is the divine Irēnē,—
    It is given, and not bought.

Strong of heart.   Be wise, be steadfast,
    Learn, endeavour, and endure ;
Blest with strength and light, in wisdom
    Make the higher purpose sure ;
Never can her heart receive thee
    Till thine own is rendered pure.

I but shone in truth above her ;
    Psyche-like, she yearned to me,
And her soul, an Aphrodite,
    Rose above the ether sea.
Love.   Love should and will inherit
    The divine Euphrosyne."

When at night, the gleaming heavens
    Throb through all their starry veins,
Oft I ponder on Orion,
    And I hear celestial strains
Passing through my soul, and flooding
    All its green immortal plains.

Then I pray for strength Promethean,
    Pray for power to endure;
Then I say, O soul, be steadfast!
    Make the lofty purpose sure;
And that love may be all-worthy,
    God of heaven, make me pure!

THE MYSTERY.

My mind is like a troubled sea
    O'er which the winds forever sweep;
Within its depths, eternally,
    My being's pulses throb and leap;
There germs of contemplation sleep,
    Like stars beyond the Milky Way,—
Like pearls within the gloomy deep,
    That never saw the light of day.

Oh, wondrous mind, how little known !
    Whence comes the thought that through my brain
Floats weirdlike as the pleasing tone
    That quickens a belovèd strain?
It may have graced some sweet refrain
    A thousand years ago, or more;
Some Norman Prince, some valiant Dane,
    May have imbibed it with their lore.

It may have strengthened Plato's soul,
    Its clarion echoes ringing through
His brain, the heaven-reaching goal
    Whence wisdom had its starry view;
It may have cheered the gifted few
    Whose minds were mints of royal song,
Who toiled where Shakespeare soared, and drew
    Down blessings from the grateful throng.

And on for ages yet to come,
    Through minds by heavenly impulse fired,
That thought may strike some scorner dumb,
    In all its regal guise attired;

Divinely blest, though uninspired,
　　Some soul may change its swift career,
Bearing the great truth, long-desired,
　　In triumph to the highest sphere.

Unbounded universe of Thought!
　　Illimitable realms of mind!
Regions of Fancy, wonder-fraught!
　　Imagination unconfined!
Temples of mystery! behind
　　Whose veils the God-appointed plan
In perfect wisdom is enshrined,
　　Beyond the pigmy reach of man:

I cannot—dare not—seek to know
　　What finite vision, to the end,
Through years of strictest search below,
　　Must ever fail to comprehend!
God! whose intents so far transcend
　　Our poor discernment, let me see
Some portion of the truths that tend
　　By slow gradations up to Thee:

That in the less imperfect years,
　　When human frailty shall have died,
When the vexed riddle of the spheres,
　　Interpreted and glorified,
Shall be as nothing to the tide
　　Of light in which Thy hidden ways
Will be revealed: I may abide
　　Thy meanest instrument of praise,
And from the broad calm ocean of Thy truth
And wisdom drinking, find eternal youth.

LOVE AND TRUTH.

Young Love sat in a rosy bower,
  Towards the close of a summer day;
At the evening's dusky hour,
  Truth bent her blessed steps that way;
      Over her face
      Beaming a grace
Never bestowed on child of clay.

Truth looked on with an ardent joy,
  Wondering Love could grow so tired;
Hovering o'er him she kissed the boy,
  When, with a sudden impulse fired,
      Exquisite pains
      Burning his veins,
Wildly he woke, as one inspired.

Eagerly Truth embraced the god,
  Filling his soul with a sense divine;
Rightly he knew the paths she trod,
  Springing from heaven's royal line;
      Far had he strayed
      From his guardian maid,
Perilling all for his rash design.

Still as they went, the tricksy youth
  Wandered afar from the maiden fair;
Many a plot he laid, in sooth,
  Wherein the maid could have no share
      Sowing his seeds,
      Bringing forth weeds,
Seldom a rose, and many a tare.

Save when the maiden was by his side,
   Love was erratic, and rarely true;
When she smiled on the graceful bride,
   Over the old world rose the new,
      Into life's skies
      Blending her dyes,
   Fairer than those of the rainbow's hue.

Sunny-eyed maidens, whom Love decoys,
   Mark well the arts of the wayward youth!
Sorrows he bringeth, disguised as joys,
   Rose-hued delights with cores of ruth;
      Learn to believe
      Love will deceive,
   Save when he comes with his guardian, Truth.

THE WREN.

Early each spring the little wren
  Came scolding to his nest of moss ;
We knew him by his peevish cry,
  He always sung so very cross.
His quiet little mate would lay
Her eggs in peace, and think all day.

He was a sturdy little wren ;
  And when he came in spring, we knew,
Or seemed to know, the flowers would grow
  To please him, where they always grew,
Among the rushes, cheerfully ;
But not a rush so straight as he !

All summer long that little wren
  Would chatter like a saucy thing ;
And in the bush attack the thrush
  That on the hawthorn perched to sing.
Like many noisy little men,
Lived, bragged, and fought that little wren.

There was a thoughtful maid, and I,
  We used to play along the shore,
Searching for shells, and culling flowers,
  As at the threshold of life's door,
Through which we had to pass, we stood,
Twin types of childish hardihood.

Year after year we gathered flowers,
    And grew apace, as children do ;
And each returning spring we marked
    The little wrens, they never grew ;
One over-quiet and sedate,
The other, a bird-reprobate.

But now the marsh is overflowed,
    The rushes rot beneath the sand ;
No spring brings back the little wrens,
    No children loiter hand in hand ;
The maiden rose-bud, pure and good,
Grown to the flower of womanhood.

GRANDPERE.

Old Grandpere sat in the corner,
　　With his grandchild on his knee,
Looking up at his wrinkled visage,
　　For his winters were ninety-three.

Fair Eleanor's locks were flaxen,
　　The old man's once were gray,
But now, they were white as the snow-drift
　　That lay on the bleak highway.

Her summers rolled on as golden
　　As waves over sunny seas;
But Grandpere could perceive no summers,
　　The winters alone were his.

He folded his arms around her,
　　Like Winter embracing Spring;
And the angels looked down from heaven,
　　And smiled on their slumbering.

But soon the angelic faces
　　Were filled with seraphic light,
As they gazed on a beauteous spirit
　　Passing up through the frosty night:

Till it stood serene before them,
　　A youth most divinely fair;
And they saw that the new-born angel
　　Was the spirit of old Grandpere.

H

ENGLAND'S HOPE AND ENGLAND'S HEIR.

England's Hope and England's Heir!
  Head and crown of Britain's glory,
Be thy future half so fair
  As her past is famed in story,
Then wilt thou be great, indeed,
  Daring, where there's cause to dare;
Greatest in the hour of need,
  England's Hope and England's Heir.

By her past, in acts supreme,
  By her present grand endeavour,
By her future, which the gleam
  Of our fond hopes brings us ever:
We can trust that thou wilt be
  Worthy of a fame so rare,
Worthy of thy destiny,
  England's Hope and England's Heir.

Be thy spirit fraught with hers,
  Queen, whom we revere and honour;
Be thine acts love's messengers,
  Brightly flashing back upon her;
Be what most her trust would deem,
  Help the answer to her prayer,
Realize her holiest dream,
  England's Hope and England's Heir.

Welcome, Prince! the land is wide,
  Wider still the love we cherish;
Love that thou shalt find, when tried,
  Is not born to droop and perish;

Welcome to our heart of hearts;
 You will find no falsehood there,
But the zeal that truth imparts,
 England's Hope and England's Heir.

Welcome to our woodland deeps,
 To our inland lakes, and rivers,
Where the rapid roars and sweeps,
 Where the brightest sunlight quivers.
Loyal souls can never fail;
 Serfdom crouches in its lair;
But our British hearts are hale,
 England's Hope and England's Heir.

ROSE.

When the evening broods quiescent
  Over mountain, vale and lea,
And the moon uplifts her crescent
  Far above the peaceful sea,
Little Rose, the fisher's daughter,
  Passes in her cedar skiff
O'er the dreamy waste of water,
  To the signal on the cliff.

Have a care, my merry maiden!
  Young Adonis though he be,
Many hearts are secret-laden
  That have trusted such as he.
Has he worth, and is he truthful?
  Thoughtless maiden rarely knows;
But, "He's handsome, brave and youthful,"
  Says the heart of little Rose.

Hark! the horn—its shrill vibrations
  Tremble through the maiden's breast,
As the sweet reverberations
  Dwindle to their whispered rest;
Sweeter far the honied sentence
  Sealing up her mind's repose;
Love as yet needs no repentance
  In the heart of little Rose.

Heaven shield thee, trusting mortal!
  Love has heaved its firstborn sigh;
But from the pellucid portal
  Of her calm, indignant eye,

Darts that make the strong man tremble
  Pierce his bosom ere he goes;
Rank and station may dissemble,
  There is truth in little Rose.

Take my hand, my fisher maiden,
  There's a grasp for thee and thine;
Constancy is love's bright Aiden,
  Self-denial is divine.
Take my hand upon this pláteau,
  Let me share thy mortal throes;
Come, dear Love! we'll build our cháteau
  In the heart of little Rose.

THE DREAMER.

Spirit of Song! whose whispers
    Delight my pensive brain,
When will the perfect harmony
    Ring through my feeble strain?

When will the rills of melody
    Be widened to a stream?
When will the bright and gladsome Day
    Succeed this morning dream?

" Mortal," the spirit whispered,
    " If thou wouldst truly win
The race thou art pursuing,
    Heed well the voice within:

And it shall gently teach thee
    To read thy heart, and know
No human strain is perfect,
    However sweet it flow.

And if thou readest truly,
    As surely shalt thou find
That truths, like rills, though diverse,
    Are choicest in their kind.

The souls of Poet-Dreamers
    Touch heaven on their way;
With the light of Song to guide them
    It should be always Day."

NIGHT AND MORNING.

The winds are piping loud to-night,
　　And the waves roll strong and high;
God pity the watchful mariner
　　Who toils 'neath yonder sky!

I saw the vessel speed away,
　　With a free, majestic sweep,.
At evening as the sun went down
　　To his palace in the deep.

An aged crone sàt on the beach,
　　And, pointing to the ship,
"She'll never return again," she said,
　　With a scorn upon her lip.

———

The morning rose tempestuous,
　　The winds blew to the shore,
There were corpses on the sands that morn,
　　But the ship came nevermore!

WITHIN THINE EYES.

Within thine eyes two spirits dwell,
  The sweetest and the purest
That ever wove Love's mystic spell,
  Or plied his arts the surest:
    No smile of morn,
    Though heaven-born,
  Nor sunshine earthward straying,
    E'er charmed the sight
    With half the light
  That round thy lips is playing.

The stars may shine, the moon may smile,
  The earth in beauty languish,
Life's sorrows these can but beguile,
  But thou canst heal its anguish.
    Thy voice, like rills
    Of silver, trills
  Such sounds of liquid sweetness,
    Each accent rolls
    Along our souls,
  In lyrical completeness.

If Friendship lend thee such a grace,
  That men nor gods may slight it,
How blest the one who views thy face
  When Love comes down to light it!
    And, oh, if he
    Who holds in fee
  Thy beauty, truth, and reason,
    A traitor prove
    To thee and Love,
  We'll spurn him for his treason.

GERTRUDE.

Underneath the maple-tree
Gertrude worked her filigree,
    All the summer long;
To sweet airs her voice was wed,
As she plied her golden thread;
Echo stealing through the grove
Filched away the words of love,
And the birds, from tree to tree,
Bore the witching melody
    Through avenues of Song.

Underneath the maple-trees
Zephyrs chant her melodies,
    All the summer long;
Words and airs no longer wed,
Death has snapped the vocal thread
Echo sleeping in the grove
Dreams of liquid airs of love,
And the birds among the trees
Fill with sweetest symphonies
    Whole avenues of Song.

FLOWERS.

Thank God I love the Flowers!
  Mute voices of the Spring,
That gladden all her bowers
  With their varied blossoming;
They weave a charm around them
  On each summer dale and bough,
For a Fairy train has bound them
  In wreaths upon her brow.

Far up along the mountain,
  And in the valleys green,
In the field, and by the fountain,
  The smiling ones are seen;
Some looking up to heaven,
  With eyes of deepest blue;
Some stooping down at even
  To quaff the sparkling dew.

And from them all there speaketh
  A language sweet and pure,
Fitted for him who seeketh
  A God's nomenclature.
As tidal pulses thrill the seas,
  And moments build the hours,
Heaven breathes her unvoiced mysteries
  In sermons from the Flowers.

THE UNATTAINABLE.

I yearn for the Unattainable;
  For a glimpse of a brighter day,
    When hatred and strife,
    With their legions rife,
  Shall forever have passed away;
    When pain shall cease,
    And the dawn of peace
  Come down from heaven above,
  And man can meet his fellow-man
  In the spirit of Christian Love.

I yearn for the Unattainable;
  For a Voice that may long be still,
    To compel the mind,
    As heaven designed,
  To work the Eternal Will;
    When the brute that sleeps
    In the heart's still deeps
  Will be changed to Pity's dove,
  And man can meet his fellow-man
  In the spirit of Perfect Love.

YEARNINGS.

I long for diviner regions,—
    The spirit would reach its goal;
Though this world hath surpassing beauty,
    It warreth against the soul.

There's a cloud in the eastern heaven;
    Beyond it, a cold gray sky;
But I know that the sun's rare radiance
    Will brighten it by and by.

In the fane of my soul is glowing
    The joy of a hope to come,
That will touch with its Memnon finger
    The lips that are cold and dumb:

Till illumed by the smile of heaven,
    And blest with a purer life,
Will the gloom that o'ershades my spirit
    Depart like a vanquished strife.

INGRATITUDE.

Full on the wave the moonlight weeps,
　To quiet its weary breast;
Cruelly cold the mad wave leaps,
　With the moonshine on its crest;
Or with scowl, or growl, to the shore it creeps,
　And sinks to its selfish rest.

Full on yon man-brute smiles the wife,
　To gladden his turbid breast;
Savagely stern he seeks the life
　Where he erewhile sought for zest;
With a curse, or worse, he ends the strife,
　And sinks to his drunken rest.

Sea! has the moon no charms for thee
　That can touch thy cruel breast?
Man! cannot woman's charity
　Give ease to thy soul oppressed?
Thou shalt flee, O sea! the moon's witchery,
　Till man has his final rest!

TRUE LOVE.

Her love is like the hardy flower
   That blooms amid the Alpine snows;
Deep-rooted in an icy bower,
   No blast can chill its sweet repose;
   But fresh as is the tropic rose,
Drenched in mellowest sunny beams,
It has as sweet delicious dreams
   As any flower that grows.

And though an avalanche came down
   And robbed it of the light of day,
That which withstood the tempest's frown
   In grief would never pine away.
   Hope might withhold her feeblest ray,
Within her bosom's snowy tomb
Love still would wear its everbloom,
   The gayest of the gay.

AN EVENING THOUGHT.

Bird of the fanciful plumage,
   That foldest thy wings in the west,
Imbuing the shimmering ocean
   With the hues of thy delicate breast,
Passing away into Dreamland,
   To visions of heavenly rest !

Spirit ! when thou art permitted
   To bask in the sunset of life ;
Serene in thine eventide splendour,
   Thy countenance victory rife ;
Leaving the world where thou'st triumphed
   Alike o'er its greatness and strife :

Thine be the destiny, spirit,
   To set like the sun in the west ;
Folding thy wings of rare plumage,
   Conscious of infinite rest ;
Heralded on to thy haven,
   The Fortunate Isles of the Blest.

A THOUGHT FOR SPRING.

I am happier for the Spring;
  For my heart is like a bird
That has many songs to sing,
  But whose voice is never heard
Till the happy year is caroling
  To the daisies on the sward.

I'd be happier for the Spring,
  Though my heart had grown so old
Like a crone 'twould sit and sing
  Its shrill runes of wintry cold;
For I'd know the year was caroling
  To the daisies on the wold.

THE SWALLOWS.

I asked the first stray swallow of the spring,
" Where hast thou been through all the winter drear ?
Beneath what distant skies did'st fold thy wing,
    Since thou wast with us here,
When Autumn's withered leaves foretold the passing
      year ?"

And it replied, " Whither has Fancy led   ·
The plumy thoughts that circle through thy brain ?
Like birds about some mountain's lofty head,
    Singing a sweet refrain :
There, without bound, I've been, and must return
      again."

SONG.—CLARA AND I.

We have a joke whenever we meet,
    Clara and I ;
Prattle and laughter, and kisses sweet,
    Clara and I.
Were I but twenty, and not two score,
Clara and I would laugh still more,
With plenty of hopeful years in store
  For Clara and I, Clara and I ;
With plenty of hopeful years in store
    For Clara and I.

We will be true as Damascus steel,
    Clara and I ;
Sealing our truth with a honied seal,
    Clara and I.
Eyes so loving, and lips of rose,
Cheeks where the dainty ripe peach grows,
And mouth where the sly god smiles jocose
  At Clara and I, Clara and I ;
And mouth where the sly god smiles jocose
    At Clara and I.

We have a kiss whenever we part,
    Clara and I ;
Grasping of hand, and flutter of heart,
    Clara and I.
Were she but twenty, and not sixteen,
Over my love she'd reign the queen,

And no fair rival should come between
My Clara and I, Clara and I ;
And no fair rival should come between
My Clara and I.

THE APRIL SNOW-STORM.—1858.

Spread lightly, virgin shower,
  Your winding-sheet of snow;
Winter has lost his power,
  But mock not at his woe.

Fall not so cold and bleak,
  Nor blow the breath of scorn;
Gently.   Thy sire is weak;
  And thou, his latest-born.

Frail type of life thou art:
  At first, pure as the snow
We come—abide—depart;
  What more, th' Immortals know.

Fall gently, virgin shower,
  Though wild the west wind raves;
Watch through this midnight hour
  Above the new-made graves!

———

Spread gently, virgin shower,
  Your winding sheet of snow;
My heart has lost its power,
  But mock not at its woe.

Fall not so cold and bleak,
  Treat not her corse with scorn;
Gently.   My heart is weak;
  She, too, was April-born.

Fall gently, virgin shower;
   The heart once strong and brave
Hath lost its wonted power;
   'Tis buried in her grave.

GOOD NIGHT.

We never say, " Good Night ;"
For our eag r lips are fleeter
Than the tongue, and a kiss is sweeter
　　Than parting words,
　　That cut like swords ;
So we always kiss Good Night.

We never say " Good Night."
Words are precious, love, why lose 'em ?
Fold them up in your maiden bosom ;
　　There let them rest,
　　Like love unconfessed,
While we kiss a sweet Good Night.

There comes a last Good Night.
Human life—not love—is fleeting ;
Heaven send many a birth-day greeting ;
　　Dim years roll on
　　To life's gray-haired dawn,
Ere we ki-s our last Good Night.

———

We've kissed our last Good Night !
Love's warm tendrils torn and bleeding,
Vain all human interceding !
　　Oh, life ! how dark !
　　Its one vital spark
Was quenched with our last GOOD NIGHT !

HOPELESS.

I think through the long, long evenings,
   Such thoughts of intensest pain,
And I hope and watch for her coming,
   But I hope and watch in vain ;
My life is a long, long journey
   Over a barren moor,
With nought but my own dark shadow
   Hastening on before.

I'm weary of all this watching,
   Aweary of life and thought ;
For there's little hope in the distance,
   And for peace—I know it not !
Oh, why must we think and shudder,
   And shudder and think again ?
When life's but a dance of shadows
   Haunting a barren plain !

Into the Silent Land.

INTO THE SILENT LAND.

I.

" Oh for a pen of light, a tongue of fire,
That every word might burn in living flame
Upon the age's brow, and leave one name
Engraven on the future !   One desire
Fills every nook and cranny of my heart ;
One hope—one sorrow—one belovèd aim !
She whose pure life was of my life a part,
As light is of the day, could she inspire
My unmelodious muse, or tune the lyre
To diapasons worthy of the theme,
How would her joy put on its robes of light,
And nestle in my bosom once again,
As when life, like an Oriental dream,
Fanned by Arabian airs, glode down the stream
To music whose remembrance is a pain.
The foot of time might trample on my strain,
But could not quench its essence.   There was might,
And majesty, and greatness in the love
She blest me with—a blessing without stain,
And that was earthly ; since her spirit-sight
Looked through the veil, and learned love's true delight,
Which sainted ministrants alone can prove
Who taste the waters of eternal love :
I pause to think how wonderful has grown
The love that was to me so wondrous here !
Chained as I am to this terrestrial sphere,
Groping my way through darkness, and alone,

Like a blind eaglet soaring towards the sun,
How would her full experience lift and cheer
The heart that never feels its duty done,
And with a girdle of pure light enzone
My flowery world of thought, and make it all her own."

Thus mused the Minstrel, for his heart was sad.
Death had bereaved him of his bride, while youth,
And looming years of future trust and truth,
Knit them together, till their souls were clad
With joy ineffable.   Love's great High Priest
Sacrificed in their hearts to Him that doeth
All things well ; and such rare, perpetual feast
Of love and truth no mortals ever had,
To keep their memories green, their lives serene and
    glad.

He sat again within the quiet room,
Where Death had snapped one golden thread of life,
And the pale hand of Sickness, sorrow-rife,
Robbed the plump cheek of childhood of its bloom ;
Where she, another Philomena, moved .
Like a fond Charity—the coming wife
Ordained to crown his being: And he loved.
The future rose before him, joy and gloom ;
For where the sunlight shone, there waved the sable
    plume.

And yet he failed not, for the coming pain ;
The coming bliss would counterbalance all.
The sight prophetic that perceived the pall,
Looked far beyond for the celestial gain.

They do not truly love who cannot yield
The mortal up at the Immortal's call,
Or fail to triumph for the soul that's sealed.
His mind was strung to one harmonious strain :
To give when God should ask, and not resign in vain.

Love was to him life's chiefest victory ;
He knew no greater, and he sought no less.
Like a green isle surrounded by the sea
That gives it health and vigour, so was he
The centre of love's sphere of perfectness ;
He breathed its heavenly atmosphere ; the key
That opened every chamber in love's court
Was in his hand ; love's mystery was his sport ;
He knelt within love's fane and worshipped there—
But not alone, for one was by his side
Whose love refined his being, filled the air
Of life's irradiated sky with light,
As the sun floods the heavens with a tide
Of renovating freshness, as the night
Is mellowed by the ample moon.
And hoping for the recompense
That would be theirs in life's approaching noon,
They built on hope's high eminence
Their airy palaces, whose magnificence
Surpassed the dreams that fancy drew,
So fair the promised land that lay within their view.

And here they lived ; just within reach of heaven.
They could put forth their hands and touch the skies
That brooded o'er the walls of chrysolite,
The airy minarets, and golden domes

Of their new home, by Love, the Maker, given,
Steeped in his brightest dyes.
All nature opened up her ponderous tomes,
Whereby they had new knowledge and new sight,
Learned greater truths, and saw the paths of light,
Mosaic-paven, which to Duty led.
And there were secrets written overhead,
In burning hieroglyphs of thought,
From which they gleaned such lessons as are taught
Only to those whom heaven, in graciousness,
Lifts in her arms with a divine caress.
Earth, like a joyous maiden whose pure soul
Is filled with sudden ecstacy, became
A fruitful Eden; and the golden bowl
That held their elixir of life was filled
To overflowing with the rarest draught
Ever by gods or men in rapture quaffed;
Till from the altar of their hearts love's flame
Passed through the veins of the world, and thrilled
The soul of the rejoicing universe,
Which became theirs, and like true neophytes
They drained the sweet nepenthe, and love's rites
Wiped from their hearts all trace of the primeval curse.

The happy months rolled on; each wedded day
A bridal; and each calm and holy eve
Strewed with rare blessings all the sunny way
Through which they passed, with so divine a joy
That in his brain would meditation weave
Love's roses into garlands of sweet song,
To deck the brow of his devoted wife.

In this their El Dorado, no alloy
Mixed with the coinage of their wedded life;
The workmen in the mint an honest throng.
No wonder, then, that with so fine a bliss
Informing every fibre of his brain,
His thoughts begat impressions such as this;
Linking their lives together with a chain
Of melody as rare as some divine refrain:

　　　Like dew to the thirsty flower,
　　　　Like sweets to the hungry bee,
　　　Is love's divinest dower,
　　　Its tenderness and power,
　　　　To thee, dear Wife! to thee.

　　　Like light to the darkened spirit,
　　　　Like oil to the turbid sea,
　　　Like truthful words to merit,
　　　Are the blessings I inherit
　　　　With thee, dear Wife! with thee.

　　　Afar in the distant ages,
　　　　Soul-ransomed, and spirit-free,
　　　I'll read all being's pages,
　　　Unread by mortal sages,
　　　　With thee, dear Wife! with thee.

None but the happy heart could carol thus;
A feather stolen from Devotion's wing,
To keep as a memento of the time
When earth met heaven, in life's duteous
And prayerful journey towards the shadowy clime;

Ere they descended from their height sublime,
Where at Love's well-filled table, banqueting,
They sat, and watched the first glad year,
Earthlike, revolving round the sun
Of their true life.   Within that sphere
Was the new Eden.   One by one
The precious moments dropped like golden sands,
And formed the solid hours.   No perilous strands
Delayed life's blissful current, as it sped
Through flowery realms with blue skies overhead,
To songs and laughter musically sweet,
As if all sorrow had forever fled;
And idylls, sung with cheerful tone,
Haunted the calm, enchanted zone
That hemmed them in,
Where, like a stately queen,
Sate Peace, beatified, serene,
The guardian, heaven-sent, of this their fair demesne:

LOVE'S ANNIVERSARY.

Like a bold, adventurous swain,
    Just a year ago to-day,
I launched my bark on a radiant main,
    And Hymen led the way :
"Breakers ahead!" he cried,
    As he sought to overwhelm
My daring craft in the shrieking tide,
But Love, like a pilot bold and tried,
    Sat, watchful, at the helm.

And we passed the treacherous shoals,
   Where many a hope lay dead,
And splendid wrecks were piled, like the ghouls
   Of joys forever fled.
Once safely over these,
   We sped by a fairy realm,
Across the bluest and calmest seas
That were ever kissed by a truant breeze,
   With Love still at the helm.

We sailed by sweet, odorous isles,
   Where the flowers and trees were one ;
Through lakes that vied with the golden smiles
   Of heaven's unclouded sun :
Still speeds our merry bark,
   Threading life's peaceful realm,
And 'tis ever morn with our marriage-lark,
For the Pilot-Love of our safety-ark
   Stands, watchful, at the helm.

II.

A beautiful land is the Land of Dreams,
   Green hills and valleys, and deep lagoons,
Swift-rushing torrents and gentle streams,
   Glassing a myriad silver moons;
Mirror-like lakelets with lovely isles,
   And verdurous headlands looking down
On the Neread shapes, whose smiles
   Were worth the price of a peaceful crown.

K

We clutch at the silvery bars
Flung from the motionless stars,
 And climb far into space,
 Defying the race
Who ride in aërial cars.

We take up the harp of the mind,
 And finger its delicate strings;
  The notes, soft and light
  As a moonbeam's flight,
Departing on viewless wings.
Afar in some fanciful bower,
 Some region of exquisite calm,
Where the starlight falls in a gleaming shower,
  We sink to repose
  On our couch of rose,
Inhaling no mortal balm.
The worlds are no longer unknown,
 We pass through the uttermost sky,
  Our eyelids are kissed
  By a gentle mist,
  And we feel the tone
  Of a calmer zone,
As if heaven were wondrous nigh.

A fanciful land is the Land of Dreams,
 Where earth and heaven are clasping hands;
  No heaven—no earth,
  But one wide, new birth,
Where Beauty and Goodness, and human worth,
Make earth of heaven and heaven of earth;
 And angels are walking on golden strands.

And the pearly gates of the universe
Of mind and fancy, opening
To the touch of the dainty finger-tips
Of elegant Peris with rose-bud lips,
Delicate, weird-like sounds are born
From the amber depths of odorous morn,
And spirits of beauty and light rehearse
    Such strains as the young immortals sing,
        When the souls of the blest
        Are borne to their rest,
On luminous pinions of light serene
To the fragrant bowers of evergreen ;
O'er the rosy plains, where the dying hours
Are changed by a spell to celestial flowers,
Where the skies have a hue no name can express,
For the tone of their passionate loveliness
    Surpasseth all human imagining.

Such was their beautiful Dream of Life ;
    Each stern reality softened down ;
Earth seemed to have ended her age of Strife,
    And Harmony reigned, her olive crown
Resting on the Parian brow
    Of the fair victor, like the gleam
Of the silvery moon on waves that flow
    Thoughtfully down the summer stream.
Such was their earnest Dream of Life !
Was it some angel, with jealous eye,
Seeing such love beneath the sky
As never yet in world or star,
Or spheral height, that reached so far
'Twas never beheld by mortal sight,

Or elsewhere, save in highest heaven,
Was duly earned, or truly given,
That leagued with the usurper, Death,
To quench the light that shone so bright
That in all the earth there was not a breath
So foul as to change their day to night?

Alone! alone!   Oh, word of fearful tone!
Well might the moon withhold her light,
The stars withdraw from human sight,
When Love was overthrown.
The Minstrel's heart how changed!
Love's principalities,
O'er which he reigned supreme,
Usurped by earth's realities;
The realm through which he ranged
Become a vanished dream!
And yet he sung, as sings
The dying swan that droops its wings
And drifts along the stream:

———

THE LIGHT IN THE WINDOW PANE.

A joy from my soul's departed,
  A bliss from my heart is flown,
As weary, weary-hearted,
  I wander alone—alone!
The night wind sadly sigheth
  A withering, wild refrain,
And my heart within me dieth
  For the light in the window pane.

The stars overhead are shining,
    As brightly as e'er they shone,
As heartless—sad—repining,
    I wander alone—alone !
A sudden flash comes streaming,
    And flickers adown the lane,
But no more for me is gleaming
    The light in the window pane.

The voices that pass are cheerful,
    Men laugh as the night winds moan ;
They cannot tell how fearful
    'Tis to wander alone—alone !
For them, with each night's returning,
    Life singeth its tenderest strain,
Where the beacon of love is burning—
    The light in the window pane.

Oh, sorrow beyond all sorrows
    To which human life is prone :
Without thee, through all the morrows,
    To wander alone—alone !
Oh, dark, deserted dwelling !
    Where Hope like a lamb was slain,
No voice from thy lone walls welling,
    No light in thy window pane.

But memory, sainted angel !
    Rolls back the sepulchral stone,
And sings like a sweet evangel :
    " No—never, never alone !

True grief has its royal palace,
    Each loss is a greater gain;
And Sorrow ne'er filled a chalice
    That Joy did not wait to drain!"

———

    " Man must be perfected
    By suffering," he said;
" And Death is but the stepping-stone, whereby
    We mount towards the gate
    Of heaven, soon or late.
Death is the penalty of life; we die,

    Because we live; and life
    Is but a constant strife
With the immortal Impulse that within
    Our bodies seeks control—
    The time-abiding Soul,
That wrestles with us—yet we fain would win.

    And what? the victory
    Would make us slaves; and we,
Who in our blindness struggle for the prize
    Of this illusive state
    Called Life, do but frustrate
The higher law—refusing to be wise."

    Rightly he knew, indeed,
    Earth's brightest paths but lead
To the true wisdom of that perfect state,
    Where Knowledge, heaven-born,
    And Love's eternal morn,
Awaiteth those who would be truly great.

With what abiding trust
He rose from out the dust,
As Death's swift chariot passed him by the way;
No visionary dream
Was his—no trifling theme—
The Soul's great Mystery before him lay:

THE SOUL.

All my mind has sat in state,
   Pond'ring on the deathless Soul:
   What must be the Perfect Whole,
When the atom is so great!

God! I fall in spirit down,
   Low as Persian to the sun;
   All my senses, one by one,
In the stream of Thought must drown.

On the tide of mystery,
   Like a waif, I'm seaward borne;
   Ever looking for the morn
That will yet interpret Thee.

Opening my blinded eyes,
   That have strove to look within,
   'Whelmed in clouds of doubt and sin,
Sinking where I dared to rise:

Could I trace one Spirit's flight,
   Track it to its final goal,
   Know that ' Spirit' meant ' the Soul, '
I must perish in the light.

All in vain I search, and cry:
   "What, O Soul, and whence art thou?"
   Lower than the earth I bow,
Stricken with the grave reply:

"Wouldst thou ope what God has sealed—
   Sealed in mercy here below?
   What is best for man to know,
Shall most surely be revealed!"

Deep on deep of mystery!
   Ask the sage, he knows no more
   Of the soul's unspoken lore
Than the child upon his knee!

Cannot tell me whence the thought
   That is passing through my mind!
   Where the mystic soul is shrined,
Wherewith all my life is fraught?

Knows not how the brain conceives
   Images almost divine;
   Cannot work my mental mine,
Cannot bind my golden sheaves.

Is he wiser, then, than I,
   Seeing he can read the stars?
   I have rode in fancy's cars
Leagues beyond his farthest sky!

Some old Rabbi, dreaming o'er
   The sweet legends of his race,
   Ask him for some certain trace
Of the far, eternal shore.

No.   The Talmud page is dark,
   Though it burn with quenchless fire ;
   And the insight must pierce higher,
That would find the vital spark.

O, my Soul! be firm and wait,
   Hoping with the zealous few,
   Till the Shekinah of the True
Lead thee through the Golden Gate.

SONNETS,

WRITTEN IN THE ORILLIA WOODS.

August, 1859.

DEDICATED

TO

𝔐𝔂 𝔉𝔯𝔦𝔢𝔫𝔡𝔰

AT

"ROCKRIDGE," ORILLIA, C. W.

SONNETS.

ALICE, I need not tell you that the Art
That copies Nature, even at its best,
Is but the echo of a splendid tone,
Or like the answer of a little child
To the deep question of some frosted sage.
For Nature in her grand magnificence,
Compared to Art, must ever raise her head
Beyond the cognizance of human minds:
This is the spirit merely; that, the soul.
We watch her passing, like some gentle dream,
And catch sweet glimpses of her perfect face;
We see the flashing of her gorgeous robes,
And, if her mantle ever falls at all,
How few Elishas wear it sacredly,
As if it were a valued gift from heaven.
God has created; we but re-create,
According to the temper of our minds;
According to the grace He has bequeathed;
According to the uses we have made
Of His good-pleasure given unto us.
And so I love my art; chiefly, because
Through it I rev'rence Nature, and improve
The tone and tenor of the mind He gave.
God sends a Gift; we crown it with high Art,

And make it worthy the bestower, when
The talent is not hidden in the dust
Of pampered negligence and venial sin,
But put to studious use, that it may work
The end and aim for which it was bestowed.
All Good is God's; all Love and Truth are His;
We are His workers; and we dare not plead
But that He gave us largely of all these,
Demanding a discreet return, that when
The page of life is written to its close
It may receive the seal and autograph
Of His good pleasure—the right royal sign
And signet of approval, to the end
That we were worthy of the gift divine,
And through it praised the Great Artificer.

 In my long rambles through Orillian woods;
Out on the ever-changing Couchiching;
By the rough margin of the Lake St. John;
Down the steep Severn, where the artist sun,
In dainty dalliance with the blushing stream,
Transcribes each tree, branch, leaf, and rock and flower,
Perfect in shape and colour, clear, distinct,
With all the panoramic change of sky—
Even as Youth's bright river, toying with
The fairy craft where Inexperience dreams,
And subtle Fancy builds its airy halls,
In blest imagination pictures most
Of bright or lovely that adorn life's banks,
With the blue vault of heaven over all;
On that serene and wizard afternoon,
As hunters chase the wild and timid deer

We chased the quiet of Medonte's shades
Through the green windings of the forest road,
Past Nature's venerable rank and file
Of primal woods—her Old Guard, sylvan-plumed—
The far-off Huron, like a silver thread,
The clue to some enchanted labyrinth,
Dimly perceived beyond the stretch of woods,
Th' approaches tinted by a purple haze,
And softened into beauty like the dream
Of some rapt seer's Apocalyptic mood;
And when at Rockridge we sat looking out
Upon the softened shadows of the night,
And the wild glory of the throbbing stars;
Where'er we bent our Eden-tinted way:
My brain was a weird wilderness of Thought:
My heart, love's sea of passion tossed and torn,
Calmed by the presence of the loving souls
By whom I was surrounded. All the while
They deemed me passing tame, and wondered when
My dreamy castle would come toppling down.
I was but driving back the aching past,
And mirroring the future. And these leaves
Of meditation are but perfumes from
The censer of my feelings; honied drops
Wrung from the busy hives of heart and brain;
Mere etchings of the artist; grains of sand
From the calm shores of that unsounded deep
Of speculation, where all thought is lost
Amid the realms of Nature and of God.

I.

My soul goes out to meet her, and my heart
Flings wide the portals of its love, and yearns
To have her enter its serene retreat.
A poor stray lamb, not wand'ring from the fold,
But all unstudied in the worldling's art,
Turning life's mintage into seeming gold,
Wherewith to purchase love and love's returns;
Unknowing that love's waters, though so sweet,
Lead to some bitter Marah.   So my soul
Goes out to meet her, and it clasps her home,
And seeks to bear her upward to the goal
At which the righteous enter.   From the dome
Of starriest Night two blest Immortals come,
To bear us spheral-ward to God's own mercy-seat.

II.

'Tis summer still, yet now and then a leaf
Falls from some stately tree.   True type of life!
How emblamatic of the pangs that grief
Wrings from our blighted hopes, that one by one
Drop from us in our wrestle with the strife
And natural passions of our stately youth.
And thus we fall beneath life's summer sun.
Each step conducts us through an opening door
Into new halls of being, hand in hand
With grave Experience, until we command
The open, wide-spread autumn fields, and store
The full ripe grain of Wisdom and of Truth.
As on life's tott'ring precipice we stand,
Our sins like withered leaves are blown about the land.

III.

Oh, holy sabbath morn ! thrice blessed day
Of solemn rest, true peace, and earnest prayer.
How many hearts that never knelt to pray
Are glad to breathe thy soul-sustaining air.
I sit within the quiet woods, and hear
The village church-bell's soft inviting sound,
And to the confines of the loftiest sphere
Imagination wings its airy round ;
A myriad spirits have assembled there,
Whose prayers on earth a sweet acceptance found.
I go to worship in Thy House, O God !
With her, thy young creation bright and fair ;
Help us to do Thy will, and not despair,
Though both our hearts should bend beneath Thy
    chastening rod.

IV.

The birds are singing merrily, and here
A squirrel claims the lordship of the woods,
And scolds me for intruding. At my feet
The tireless ants all silently proclaim
The dignity of labour. In my ear
The bee hums drowsily; from sweet to sweet
Careering, like a lover weak in aim.
I hear faint music in the solitudes;
A dreamlike melody that whispers peace
Imbues the calmy forest, and sweet rills
Of pensive feeling murmur through my brain,
Like ripplings of pure water down the hills
That slumber in the moonlight. Cease, oh, cease!
Some day my weary heart will coin these into pain.

V.

Blest Spirit of Calm that dwellest in these woods !
Thou art a part of that serene repose
That ofttimes lingers in the solitudes
Of my lone heart, when the tumultuous throes
Of some vast Grief have borne me to the earth.
For I have fought with Sorrow face to face;
Have tasted of the cup that brings to some
A frantic madness and delirious mirth,
But prayed and trusted for the light to come,
To break the gloom and darkness of the place.
Through the dim aisles the sunlight penetrates,
And nature's self rejoices; heaven's light
Comes down into my heart, and in its might
My soul stands up and knocks at God's own temple-
    gates.

VI.

Through every sense a sweet balm permeates,
As music strikes new tones from every nerve.
The soul of Feeling enters at the gates
Of Intellect, and Fancy comes to serve
With fitting homage the propitious guest.
Nature, erewhile so lonely and oppressed,
Stands like a stately Presence, and looks down
As from a throne of power. I have grown
Full twenty summers backwards, and my youth
Is surging in upon me till my hopes
Are as fresh-tinted as the checkered leaves
That the sun shines through. All the future opes
Its endless corridors, where time unweaves
The threads of Error from the golden warp of Truth.

VII.

Our life is like a forest, where the sun
Glints down upon us through the throbbing leaves ;
The full light rarely finds us.   One by one,
Deep rooted in our souls, there springeth up
Dark groves of human passion, rich in gloom,
At first no bigger than an acorn-cup.
Hope threads the tangled labyrinth, but grieves
Till all our sins have rotted in their tomb,
And made the rich loam of each yearning heart
To bring forth fruits and flowers to new life.
We feel the dew from heaven, and there start
From some deep fountain little rills whose strife
Is drowned in music.   Thus in light and shade
We live, and move, and die, through all this earthly
　　　glade.

VIII.

Above where I am sitting, o'er these stones,
The ocean waves once heaved their mighty forms;
And vengeful tempests and appalling storms
Wrung from the stricken sea portentous moans,
That rent stupendous icebergs, whose huge heights
Crashed down in fragments through the startled
    nights.
Change, change, eternal change in all but God !
Mysterious nature ! thrice mysterious state
Of body, soul, and spirit !   Man is awed,
But triumphs in his littleness.   A mote,
He specks the eye of the age and turns to dust,
And is the sport of centuries.   We note
More surely nature's ever-changing fate;
Her fossil records tell how she performs her trust.

IX.

Another day of rest, and I sit here
Among the trees, green mounds, and leaves as sere
As my own blasted hopes.   There was a time
When Love and perfect Happiness did chime
Like two sweet sounds upon this blessed day;
But one has flown forever,. far away
From this poor Earth's unsatisfied desires
To love eternal, and the sacred fires
With which the other lighted up my mind
Have faded out and left no trace behind,
But dust and bitter ashes.   Like a bark
Becalmed, I anchor through the midnight dark,
Still hoping for another dawn of Love.
Bring back my olive branch of Happiness, O dove!

X.

Poor snail, that toilest at my weary feet,
Thou, too, must have thy burden! Life is sweet,
If we would make it so.   How vast a load
To carry all its days along the road
Of its serene existence!   Christian-like,
It toils with patience, seeking sweet repose
Within itself when wearied with the throes
Of its life-struggle.   The low sounds that strike
Upon the ear in wafts of melody,
Are cruel mockeries, O snail, of thee.
The cricket's chirp, the grasshopper's shrill tone,
The locust's jarring cry, all mock thy lone
And dumb-like presence.   May this heart of mine,
When tried, put on a resignation such as thine.

XI.

Oh, that I were the spirit of these wilds!
I'd make the zephyrs dance for my delight,
And lead a life as happy as a child's.
Echo should tremble with unfeigned affright,
And mock its own weird answers.   I would kiss
Eliza's cheek, and touch her lips with dew
Stol'n from the scented rose.   And Carrie's laugh
Should be a portion of the silver rills'
Sweet music, breathed mellifluously through
The hearts of generations.   She should quaff
The nectar of inspired song, and thrills
Of sweet remembrances of her should strew
The woodland air, as sand-grains strew the shore ;
And these two hearts should be my joy for evermore.

XII.

The moon shone down on fair Eliza's face,
And made it beautiful.   No fitter place
Could she have chosen for her gracious smile ;
For as she sat there in the languid light,
Methought I'd found a soul as free from guile
As ever came from God.   Oh, favored Night !
Oh, mild, impassioned moon and starry spheres !
To gaze upon her through the silent years
Without rebuke.   But I have looked within,
And found the truest beauty ; have laid bare
A spiritual excellence as rare
As ever mortal being hoped to win.
Heart, mind, and soul, I analysed them all,
And saw where heaven kept divinest carnival.

XIII.

I've almost grown a portion of this place;
I seem familiar with each mossy stone;
Even the mimble chipmunk passes on,
And looks, but never scolds me. Birds have flown
And almost touched my hand; and I can trace
The wild bees to their hives. I've never known
So sweet a pause from labour. But the tone
Of a past sorrow, like a mournful rill
Threading the heart of some melodious hill,
Or the complainings of the whippoorwill,
Passes through every thought, and hope, and aim.
It has its uses; for it cools the flame
Of ardent love that burns my being up—
Love, life's celestial pearl, diffused through all its cup.

XIV.

There is no sadness here.   Oh, that my heart
Were calm and peaceful as these dreamy groves !
That all my hopes and passions, and deep loves,
Could sit in such an atmosphere of peace,
Where no unholy impulses would start
Responsive to the throes that never cease
To keep my spirit in such wild unrest.
'Tis only in the struggling human breast
That the true sorrow lives.   Our fruitful joys
Have stony kernels hidden in their core.
Life in a myriad phases passeth here,
And death as various—an equal poise ;
Yet all is but a solemn change—no more ;
And not a sound save joy pervades the atmosphere.

XV.

Last night I heard the plaintive whippoorwill,
And straightway Sorrow shot his swiftest dart.
I know not why, but it has chilled my heart
Like some dread thing of evil.   All night long
My nerves were shaken, and my pulse stood still,
And waited for a terror yet to come
To strike harsh discords through my life's sweet song.
Sleep came—an incubus that filled the sum
Of wretchedness with dreams so wild and chill
The sweat oozed from me like great drops of gall;
An evil spirit kept my mind in thrall,
And rolled my body up like a poor scroll
On which is written curses that the soul
Shrinks back from when it sees some hellish carnival.

XVI.

My footsteps press where, centuries ago,
The Red Men fought and conquered; lost and won.
Whole tribes and races, gone like last year's snow,
Have found the Eternal Hunting-Grounds, and run
The fiery gauntlet of their active days,
Till few are left to tell the mournful tale:
And these inspire us with such wild amaze
They seem like spectres passing down a vale
Steeped in uncertain moonlight, on their way
Towards some bourn where darkness blinds the day,
And night is wrapped in mystery profound.
We cannot lift the mantle of the past:
We seem to wander over hallowed ground:
We scan the trail of Thought, but all is overcast.

XVII.

THERE WAS A TIME—and that is all we know!
No record lives of their ensanguined deeds:
The past seems palsied with some giant blow,
And grows the more obscure on what it feeds.
A rotted fragment of a human leaf;
A few stray skulls; a heap of human bones!
These are the records—the traditions brief—
'Twere easier far to read the speechless stones.
The fierce Ojibwas, with tornado force,
Striking white terror to the hearts of braves!
The mighty Hurons, rolling on their course,
Compact and steady as the ocean waves!
The stately Chippewas, a warrior host!
Who were they?—Whence?—And why? no human
     tongue can boast!

XVIII.

I do not wonder that the Druids built
Their sacred altars in the sacred groves.
Fit place to worship God.   The native guilt
Of our poor weak humanity behoves
That we should set aside no little part
Of the devotion of the yearning heart
To rest and peace, as typical of that
Sweet tranquil rest to which the good aspire.
Calm thoughts are as the purifying fire
That burns the useless dross from life's mixed gold,
And lights the torch of mind.   While grasping at
The shadow for the substance, youth grows old,
And groves of palm spring up in every heart—
Temples to God, wherein we pray and sit apart.

XIX.

How my heart yearns towards my friends at home!
Poor suffering souls, whose lives are like the trees,
Bent, crushed, and broken in the storm of life!
A whirlwind of existence seems to roam
Through some poor hearts continually.   These
Have neither rest nor pause ; one day is rife
With tempest, and another dashed with gloom ;
And the few rays of light that might illume
Their thorny path are drenched with tearful rain.
Yet these pure souls live not their lives in vain ;
For they become as spiritual guides
And lights to others ; rising with the tides
Of their full being into higher spheres,
Brighter and brighter still through all the coming
     years.

XX

I sat within the temple of her heart,
And watched the living Soul as it passed through,
Arrayed in pearly vestments, white and pure.
The calm, immortal Presence made me start.
It searched through all the chambers of her mind
With one mild glance of love, and smiled to view
The fastnesses of feeling, strong—secure,
And safe from all surprise.   It sits enshrined
And offers incense in her heart, as on
An altar sacred unto God.   The dawn
Of an imperishable love passed through
The lattice of my senses, and I, too,
Did offer incense in that solemn place—
A woman's heart made pure and sanctified by Grace.

XXI.

Intense young soul, that takest hearts by storm,
And chills them into sorrow with a look!
Some minds are open as a well-read book;
But here the leaves are still uncut—unscanned,
The volume clasped and sealed, and all the warm
And passionate exuberance of love
Held in submission to these threadbare flaws,
And creeds of weaknesses, poor human laws.
Stand up erect—nay kneel—for from above
God's light is streaming on thee.   Fashion's daws
May fawn and flatter like a cringing pack
Of servile hounds beneath the keeper's hand,
But these are not thy peers; they drive thee back:
Urge on the car of Thought, and take a higher
stand!

XXII.

Dark, dismal day—the first of many such !
The wind is sighing through the plaintive trees,
In fitful gusts of a half-frenzied woe ;
Affrighted clouds the hand might almost touch,
Their black wings bend so mournfully and low,
Sweep through the skies like night-winds o'er the seas.
There is no chirp of bird through all the grove,
Save that of the young fledgeling rudely flung
From its warm nest; and like the clouds above
My soul is dark, and restless as the breeze
That leaps and dances over Couchiching.
Soon will the last duett be sweetly sung ;
But through the years to come our hearts will ring
With memories, as dear as time and love can bring.

AU REVOIR.

That morn our hearts were like artesian wells,
Both deep and calm, and brimming with pure love.
And in each one, like to an April day,
Truth smiled and wept, while Courage wound his
    horn,
Dispatching echoes that are whispering still
Through all the vacant chambers of our souls;
While Sorrow sat with drooped and aimless wing,
Within the solitary fane of thought.
We wished some warlike Joshua were there
To make the sun stand still, or to put back
The dial to the brighter side of time.
A cloud hung over Couchiching; a cloud
Eclipsed the merry sunshine of our hearts.
We needed no philosopher to teach
That laughter is not always born of joy.
"All's for the best," the fair Eliza said;
And we derived new courage from her lips,
That spake the maxim of her trusting heart.
We even smiled, at some portentous sign
That signified—well, if it turn out true,
Then, I'll believe it.   Heaven works in signs
More parting words, more lingering farewells,
Pressure of hands, and thrilling touch of lips,
A waving of white handkerchiefs, and Love
Grew prayerful, and knelt down, and wept
His scattered rosary of human hearts.

Soon looking back, we saw where Ramah lay;
Cold, wan, and cheerless as the race it holds.
And as we neared the Lake the sun came forth,
As tardily as if the sluggard day
Had slept more soundly for the piping storm,
That, veering round, had flung its challenge out
In sullen menace to the western sky,
Now black with clouds.   A flash, a muffled roll
Of elemental passion, broke the spell,
And down on Simcoe fell the sudden rain,
Veiling the gloomy landscape from our sight.
Throughout the changeful day, alternate cloud
And sunshine left their traces on our hearts,
Until the evening reared its dreamy piles
Of cloud-built châteaux steeped in gorgeous tints,
That from celestial censers are outpoured
When the grand miracle of sunset draws
Our souls, all yearning with a joy divine,
To share the fleeting glory, ere it goes
To glean new splendors for the ruby morn.
'Tis ever thus with true impassioned love:
Love's sun, like that of day, may set, and set,
It hath as bright a rising in the morn.
True love has no gray hairs; his golden locks
Can never whiten with the snows of time.
Sorrow lies drear on many a youthful heart,
Like snow upon the evergreens; but love
Can gather sweetest honey by the way,
E'en from the carcass of some prostrate grief.
We have been spoiled with blessings.   Though the
    world

Holds nothing dearer than the hope that's fled,
God ever opens up new founts of bliss—   .
Spiritual Bethsaidas where the soul
Can wash the earth-stains from its fevered loins.
We carve our sorrows on the face of joy,
Reversing the true image ; we are weak
Where strength is needed most, and most is given.

Thus musing, as they chatted in the train,
The whistle broke my reverie, as one
Might be awakened from a truthful dream.
The city gas-lights flashed into our eyes ;
And we, half-shrinking from the glare and din,
Thought but of two more partings on the morn,
When Love should be enfettered, hand and foot,
For the long æon of a human year.

THE END.

THE "ST. LAWRENCE AND THE SAGUENAY."

OPINIONS OF THE PRESS.

MRS. SUSANNA MOODIE.

BELLEVILLE, July 28th, 1856.

SIR,—Accept my sincere thanks for the volume of beautiful Poems with which you have favored me. If the world receives them with as much pleasure as they have been read by me, your name will rank high among the gifted Sons of Song. If a native of Canada, she may well be proud of her Bard, who has sung in such lofty strains the natural beauties of his native land. Wishing you all the fame you so richly deserve, I subscribe myself, your sincere admirer.

To Mr. Charles Sangster.   SUSANNA MOODIE.

REV. J. MACGEORGE.

Amongst the very few Bards which Canada has yet produced, Mr. Sangster occupies the very first rank, and he will even occupy a prominent position in the literary annals of our Province.

LONDON NATIONAL MAGAZINE.

Western Canada is enabled to boast, and does boast somewhat loudly, of Charles Sangster, who has celebrated in Spenserian Stanzas the beauties and the sublimities of the St. Lawrence and the Saguenay. Well may the Canadians be proud of such contributions to their infant literature ; well may they be forward to recognize his lively imagination, his bold masterly style, and the fulness of his imagery. * * * * There is much of the spirit of Wordsworth in this writer, only the tone is religious instead of being philosophical. * * * * In some sort, and according to his degree, he may be regarded as the Wordsworth of Canada.

His whole soul seems steeped in love and poesy, and finds utterance in expression generally eloquent, bold and musical. He is thoroughly sentimental, teeming with ideas of the sublime and beautiful, and bears evident marks of enthusiastic poetical conception. Mr. Sangster is a poet of no mean order, and his volume is far the most respectable contribution of Poetry that has yet been made to the infant literature of Canada.—*Huron Signal.*

We hail the publication of these Poems, to which we readily invite attention. They are chiefly upon topics incidental to British America; betray considerable talent, and no slight poetic skill and taste, while to their good feeling and admirable tone we give our warmest testimony.—*Canadian (London) News.*

Mr. Sangster, in his description of the St. Lawrence and the Saguenay has vividly pourtrayed the Scenery through which they pass; his book is destined to create a great sensation, and should be in the hands of every tourist who visits, or may have visited, the beautiful scenery he so charmingly depicts.—*Toronto Colonist.*

These Poems are written in a bold masterly style, full of imagery, and displaying ability of no ordinary kind. Mr. Sangster is a Poet, in the true sense of the term, and leads his readers in burning language of inspiration from Nature up to Nature's God.—*Ottawa Times.*

This is a book that, as a Canadian, we are proud of. The subject upon which it treats is one well worthy the high talents of the Author. We are glad the volume has been published; it is a great addition to the literary products of the Province. To tourists it is indispensable. As they pass along on their tour of pleasure over these two rivers, it would be a treat to read his chaste and classic muse.—*Montreal Pilot.*

The material of "Pleasant Memories" is original and excellent. Mr. Sangster is something more than one of the mob of gentlemen who write with ease. We should be glad to hear from him again.—*New York Albion.*

OPINIONS OF THE PRESS.

The Poem entitled "The St. Lawrence and the Saguenay" is a master piece; and in fact the whole book breathes the spirit of a master mind. It is in every way creditable to Mr. Sangster, and shows unmistakably that he is a Poet of decided ability, of whom Canada, his native place, ought to be proud.—*Ottawa Monarchist.*

The description of the Thousand Isles is very fine, the Lyric to the Isles very musical and beautiful; there are many fine passages in the description of the Saguenay.—*Montreal Gazette.*

A writer who will yet make his mark in the literary world.—*Buffalo Republic.*

Purity pervades every line, and pure thoughts expressed in chaste and glowing words blend in the harmony of the measure. His Poetry breathes of that faith which penetrates the unseen.—*Utica Herald.*

The work is essentially Canadian; but its strongest claim is its own intrinsic merits. The spirit, style and sentiment are on the whole eminently Poetical.—*Newburg Index.*

What we most admire in Mr. Sangster is his warm and ardent love for the beautiful and the good, and his never-failing charity; that he possesses poetical talent in a high degree any one capable of judging with allow. His reverence of the God-like, his love of the beautiful, his adoration of the true, commend his first breathings in the world of authorship to every right-thinker.—*Kingston Commercial Advertiser.*

We hail this contribution to the scanty store of Canadian Literature, and we congratulate Kingston in having in its midst one possessed of poetical talent in so high a degree.—*Kingston News.*

These Poems as a whole are every way worthy the Genius of a true-born poet like Mr. Sangster, our Native Bard; the public may well afford to patronize the best the country has produced.—*Hamilton Spectator.*

Mr. Sangster is a Canadian Poet of no inconsiderable talent. The portions of the larger Poem, "The St. Lawrence and the Saguenay," which we have perused, give us a very favorable opinion of the book. Mr. Sangster possesses a lively imagination, united to good descriptive powers, and is likely to make himself widely known as a genuine friend of the Muses.—*Toronto Globe.*

In "The St. Lawrence and the Saguenay," there breathes a spirit of description which might do credit to an author of greater fame.—*Chatham Advertiser.*

This volume of Poems is a credit to Canadian Literature.—*British Whig.*

A Canadian Poet, whose poems are far above mediocrity—whose songs are of Canada—her mountains, maidens, manners, morals, lakes, rivers, valleys, seasons, woods, forests, and aborigines, her faith and hope, merits encouragement. Will he get it?—*McKenzie's Message.*

www.ingramcontent.com/pod-product-compliance
Lightning Source LLC
Chambersburg PA
CBHW031059280326
41928CB00049B/1139